Union Public Library

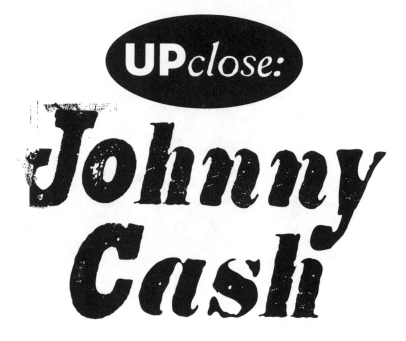

UPclose:

Johnny Cash

a twentieth-century life by
ANNE E. NEIMARK

Union Public Library

VIKING

To Marilyn—my soul sister on every journey

—A.N.(E.)

VIKING

Published by Penguin Group

Penguin Young Readers Group, 345 Hudson Street, New York, New York 10014, U.S.A.

Penguin Group (Canada), 90 Eglinton Avenue East, Suite 700, Toronto, Ontario, Canada M4P 2Y3 (a division of Pearson Penguin Canada Inc.)

Penguin Books Ltd, 80 Strand, London WC2R 0RL, England

Penguin Ireland, 25 St Stephen's Green, Dublin 2, Ireland (a division of Penguin Books Ltd)

Penguin Group (Australia), 250 Camberwell Road, Camberwell, Victoria 3124, Australia (a division of Pearson Australia Group Pty Ltd)

Penguin Books India Pvt Ltd, 11 Community Centre, Panchsheel Park, New Delhi – 110 017, India

Penguin Group (NZ), 67 Apollo Drive, Mairangi Bay, Auckland 1311, New Zealand (a division of Pearson New Zealand Ltd)

Penguin Books (South Africa) (Pty) Ltd, 24 Sturdee Avenue, Rosebank, Johannesburg 2196, South Africa

Penguin Books Ltd, Registered Offices: 80 Strand, London WC2R 0RL, England

First published in 2007 by Viking, a division of Penguin Young Readers Group

10 9 8 7 6 5 4 3 2 1

Copyright © Anne E. Neimark, 2007

All rights reserved

LIBRARY OF CONGRESS CATALOGING-IN-PUBLICATION DATA

Neimark, Anne E., date–

Up close : Johnny Cash / by Anne E. Neimark. — 1st ed.

p. cm.

ISBN-13: 978-0-670-06215-7 (hardcover)

1. Cash, Johnny. 2. Country musicians—United States—Biography—Juvenile literature. I. Title.

ML3930.C27E38 2007

782.421642092—dc22

2006010198

7/07

Printed in the U.S.A.

Set in Goudy

Book design by Jim Hoover

PHOTO CREDITS

Page 16 copyright © Associated Press, JOHNNY CASH COLLECTION

Pages 20, 32, 92, 142, 130 copyright © Les Leverett

Pages 57, 74 copyright © MICHAELOCHSARCHIVES.COM

Page 67 copyright © Morris Abernathy/Corbis

Page 108 copyright © Time Life Pictures/Getty Images

Page 160 copyright © Bettmann/CORBIS

Page 189 copyright © Associated Press, AP

But I'll try to carry off a little darkness

on my back,

'til things are brighter, I'm the Man in

Black.

—Johnny Cash, "Man in Black"

AVAILABLE UP CLOSE TITLES:

RACHEL CARSON by Ellen Levine

JOHNNY CASH by Anne E. Neimark

ROBERT F. KENNEDY by Marc Aronson

OPRAH WINFREY by Ilene Cooper

FUTURE UP CLOSE TITLES:

ELLA FITZGERALD by Tanya Stone

ELVIS PRESLEY by Wilborn Hampton

JOHN STEINBECK by Milton Meltzer

FRANK LLOYD WRIGHT by Jan Adkins

CONTENTS

FOREWORD

IN SUMMER 2004, I drove from Chicago to Nashville—a bedrock city of country music. I hungered to see some of what Johnny Cash saw, track down a few of his special haunts, and maybe feel his music even deeper in my bones. It's said that people who don't like country music are still thrilled by Johnny Cash's voice, which can reach the rafters and make their eyes pop with awe. That voice, full of power and portent, lets us in to learn what life can do for us—or to us.

The sound of Johnny's voice has always stopped me in my tracks. Besides, he was an epitome of the gritty hero of stout heart who, faced with what seemed like insurmountable odds, had surmounted them anyway. I'd wanted to write about him for years.

On Nashville's Fifth Street, I parked at the Ryman Auditorium, a converted church that, in 1943, became home to the Grand Old Opry, the first center of country music after its hard-knock birth in America's rural South. The Opry, where Johnny won over audiences—and once got in big trouble—has moved half an hour away to Opryland, but the Ryman's faded red bricks and arched windows hearken back to the fiddles, guitars, and banjos of country-music history. Nearby is the sleek Country Music Hall of Fame. Inside, I remembered that, for Johnny, being the youngest living person inducted into this hall of fame was his most prized tribute—even in the face of Grammy, MTV, CMA, and BMI awards, and being inducted into the Rock and Roll Hall of Fame. He recorded 1,500 songs on over 500 albums (counting just American and European releases), sold over 50 million records, and placed at least two singles on the country charts for thirty-eight consecutive years. Yet he was as welcome at Carnegie Hall as he was at the Grand Old Opry.

On Nashville's 16th and 17th avenues, on famed Music Row, I wandered as Johnny had among old, face-lifted houses and buildings of more modern vintage, all given over to music and film production studios and offices.

Johnny and June Carter Cash's Hendersonville house, twenty miles north of Nashville, sprawls onto acres of rolling land. Leaning from a low border wall are flowers, stuffed animals, and small American flags, mementos from grieving, devoted fans. Behind the house is Johnny's pier on Old Hickory Lake where he fished with his son, John Carter Cash.

Close to spitting distance away is the House of Cash, now closed, where many of Johnny's songs were recorded, business happened, and tourists bought gifts. In a lot to the left of the building is a rickety old train depot, once located in nearby Amqui, which Johnny had moved when it was going to be destroyed. How like him to rescue something abandoned.

At my journey's end, I stood by Johnny's and June's graves in Hendersonville Memorial Gardens Cemetery. Carved into the black granite headstone are two song titles—I WALK THE LINE (Johnny) and WILDWOOD FLOWER (June). Startled, I counted nine quarters splayed over Johnny's grave—dropped, apparently, by visitors with no flowers. I opened my wallet to find a quarter. Kneeling, I added it to the group, realizing that even if those quarters were a strange gravesite bounty, they were a genuine badge of honor. Aside from their "cash value," they gave a riveting reminder of Johnny Cash. He'd been the Man in Black, forging his raw, honest songs out of childhood poverty, tragedy, and backbreaking toil, carrying them to millions of fans from every culture and background. He'd always stood up defiantly for what he believed; he "gave no quarter" to those who opposed him. Yes, he could pray, but, oh, could he rumble.

Driving out of Nashville, guitars in storefront windows flashing by my windshield, I felt Johnny's voice like thick, steaming black coffee that pours down your throat—past any bones—into your sinew and soul. Sing on, Johnny. Who could ever stop you?

"The thing I love about Johnny Cash is the sound of his voice, the physical sound of his voice. It's like buyin' a book called, like, y'know, America . . ."

—Rick Manitoba, lead singer, the Dictators

"He'll never die or be forgotten, even by persons not born yet—especially those persons—and that is forever."   —Bob Dylan, singer/songwriter

INTRODUCTION

ON JANUARY 13, 1968, Johnny Cash—the Man in Black—shocked the world and made music history by recording a live album in front of two thousand of California's most dangerous prison inmates. Years before, in the air force, he had written his famous song, "Folsom Prison Blues," and at age thirty-five he took—along with his raw nerve—his sound crew and equipment, and his popular backup singers and guitarists, into maximum-security Folsom State Prison in Represa, California. Looming atop forty acres, the stone prison contained five massive cell blocks.

Johnny believed inmates often got a "raw deal"— abused by brutal guards and wardens, left to rot, unrehabilitated, in grubby cells. He fought for prison reform. He also found a link deep inside himself with

Johnny performing for prisoners at Folsom Prison in California, January 13, 1968. The concert was recorded for his live album Johnny Cash at Folsom Prison.

convicts who had lashed out against society in anger or despair.

Under the pitched roof of the dining hall, where the tables were nailed to the floor, Johnny stood at a microphone and stared straight into the eyes of the convicts. Rifle-toting guards paced nearby, and prison rules kept the neon lights blazing during the whole performance.

The menace of rifles, however, couldn't stop what exploded that day in the fever-pitched exchange between singer and prisoners: jokes that were hilarious and jokes that cut off breath at the throat; songs of murder, love, loneliness, death, and . . . God. All recorded on the spot by technicians from Columbia Records. Yells, screams, clapping, foot-stamping, and howls of approval filled the dining hall. Johnny Cash was so famous, every inmate knew his story—actually *liked* his story. Cash might not have done real prison time, but he was the "real thing." He wore his trademark black and pounded out his songs; he had survived both broken bones and broken promises. "I don't pretend," he said, "to be anything I'm not."

Johnny Cash at Folsom Prison became one of the

most vibrant testimonies to Johnny's spectacular gifts. The album sold over six million copies and won a Grammy for its liner notes in which Johnny wrote of a prisoner sitting on a steel, mattress-less cot, watching a cockroach but not killing it, letting the cockroach have a chance to crawl under the cell door to freedom. The album cemented Johnny's image as an outlaw, as someone who didn't cave in to authority. In 1969, he sold more records in the U.S. than the Beatles.

Prisons and churches would always be waterholes of wisdom for Johnny Cash, reminders of the tug-of-war between sin and redemption. "He was a poet," said his daughter Rosanne, "who worked in the dirt." His life—rough, earthy, creative, and honest, rising from sorrows like a sometimes tattered, mostly triumphant phoenix—is a song to sing again and again.

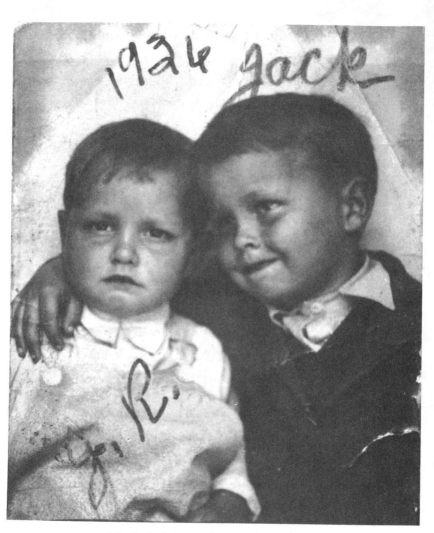

J.R. Cash (left) with his brother Jack, 1936.

ONE

THE FLATBED TRUCK sloshed and jolted down an Arkansas road. Ice-crusted mud holes grabbed at the wheels. A black tarpaulin, pocked with freezing sleet, covered the truck bed, shielding four passengers, a few pieces of unpainted furniture, and burlap bags stuffed with clothes. Ray Cash hoped he wasn't taking his family on a wild goose chase. He and most other farmers across America's farm belt, six years after being blindsided by the Great Depression—the economic collapse of 1929—were still out of work, out of money, and often out of hope.

Ray had squeezed his wife, Carrie, and two daughters, Louise and baby Reba, into the warm cab next to the disgruntled truck driver. The oldest Cash child, fourteen-year-old Roy, rode under the tarp with his father and two younger brothers, Jack and J.R. Ray had thought of naming J.R. "John," but instead had talked Carrie into the random initials. As it turned out, three-year-old J.R., born February 26, 1932, was nicknamed "Shoo-Doo." Later, he would be called Johnny.

Peeking out from the tarp, his teeth chattering, Johnny saw icicles cracking off cypress trees. The family had left a "bare-bones . . . three rooms in a row" shanty in Kingsland, Arkansas, for the cold, 250-mile journey to a five-room house in Dyess. They were part of President Franklin Roosevelt's "New Deal" to rescue a Depression-whipped country. Under the Federal Emergency Relief Association, or FERA, the U.S. government had bought cheap land in forty-six sites to relocate starving families.

The value of Ray Cash's cotton crop had plummeted in Kingsland from $150 per five-hundred-pound bale to $25—a disaster. Odd jobs (fifteen cents an hour), like cutting wood, laying railroad track, or clearing swampland, vanished, even when Ray hopped freights on the nearby Cotton Belt Railway to find work in other towns, hiding on the "blinds" between cars or, more dangerously, on underneath rods. J.R. would listen for the 5:30 A.M. whistle of "Old 90," hoping his daddy might jump from the blinds to bring home three or four dollars. Without money, there were no bullets for shooting squirrels, rabbits, coons, or possum, the family's main source of food.

On a friend's radio, Ray Cash had heard the government announcement about Arkansas relocation. Five hundred farm families would be moved to sixteen thousand acres of overgrown Mississippi Delta land, good for cotton, in the state's northeast corner. Colonization Project Number One—called "Dyess" after W. R. Dyess, the program's overseer—was laid out like sixteen wheel spokes. Relief workers had laid roads, built houses, and dug drainage ditches. Each farmer's task was clearing twenty acres of strangling vines, trees, wildcats, and poisonous snakes. A house, barn, chicken coop, mule, cow, moving expenses, and $253.59 in "doodlum" (vouchers) for supplies would be provided. But not for free. Payback must begin out of sales from the first cotton crops. All residents would have a stake in Dyess, sharing in profits or losses. Ray Cash, his pockets empty, applied for relocation. Because of his reputation as a strong worker, he was one of only five farmers chosen from Cleveland County.

When night fell on the Cashes' March 23, 1935, journey, the road was so slippery that driving had to stop until morning. Carrie, hugging baby Reba, wiped away tears over the uncertain future. Then, seeking her usual comfort, she whispered a prayer and began singing an old gospel song. From under the tarp, Johnny's small voice joined his mother's on "I Am Bound for the Promised Land." Back in Kingsland, Carrie Cash had often cried and sung. To Johnny, on that icy night on the hazardous road, "it all sounded the same."

By noon the next day, in Dyess at last, the truck couldn't navigate storm waters on Road Three where the green-trimmed, white house had been assembled in sixteen hours by a crew of ten. Hoisting Johnny atop his shoulders, Ray led Carrie and the children across the waterlogged land and tangled underbrush to the front door of the house. The last hundred yards, as Johnny would recall, were full of "thick black Arkansas mud—gumbo, we called it." The mud sucked at shoe bottoms like quicksand.

Sleet and mud traveled indoors on the meager furnishings that Ray carried from the truck. The older children went to forage in the barn for firewood; a kerosene lamp (electricity wouldn't come to Dyess for ten years) would be bought with doodlum at the community store. Johnny—thin, brown-eyed, with a mop of dark hair—was suddenly afraid of the newness. Shivering, he stayed by his older brother Jack's heels. Jack, he would say, was his "protector; I was the skinny one, and he looked after me."

Johnny was not alone in wanting protection. By sundown, the wind crashed through the front and back porches, doors rattled on their hinges, and Ray glimpsed a wildcat clawing at the empty chicken coop. Not to worry, he joked. Wildcats were safer guests than the panthers he'd been told roamed the Dyess countryside. Pulling on his worn hip-waders, Ray went out in the dark to walk the land that was to be cotton fields. Arms intertwined, Johnny and Jack watched their father march like a hardy soldier to what Johnny called "real jungle."

An hour later, when Ray tramped back into the house, the sight of him made Carrie gasp. Her husband's clothes were soaked, his face was filthy, and blood dripped from cuts on his neck. He had fallen, he said, into a stump hole—made, probably, from dynamite blasting of trees at the rear of the property. Both Carrie and Louise cried while Roy put on a brave front as eldest son. Jack, his grip tighter around Johnny, was wide-eyed. But Ray just shook his head at his family's concern. "We've got some good land," he said simply.

All seven Cashes spent the night on the floor in House No. 266, lying on damp coats and blankets. Carrie, who played piano, guitar, and fiddle, tried softly singing the children to sleep, turning once more to the gospel music loved by her grandfather, a Baptist minister, and her father, song master at the Crossroads Methodist Church in Kingsland. After another rendition of "I Am Bound for the Promised Land," she sang "What Would You Give in Exchange for Your Soul?"

Three-year-old Johnny shut his eyes. Curled onto his blanket, toes rubbing against Jack's knees, he tried not to think of panthers in the jungle. Instead, he let the words and melody of the song about the promised land warm him like honey. Maybe the newness in Dyess wasn't so bad. Maybe his daddy didn't have to jump off trains anymore, and poor families wouldn't knock at the door like they did back in Kingsland, begging for hot biscuits. And maybe, Johnny told himself, Dyess, with its mud and cold and its bad stump hole that swallowed you up—and made you bleed!—just might be a cross-your-heart promise.

Spreading like the mushrooms along the drainage ditches, Dyess grew bigger almost before you could blink. By 1936, a gas station, garage, school, and two churches appeared, along with a cannery, blacksmith shop, harness shop, hospital, library, and a café where dinner cost thirty-five cents.

Beneath a scorching Arkansas sun, Ray and Roy Cash worked and sweated from sunup to sunset, clearing and plowing three acres of land—two for cotton, one for family food. They used axes and saws to cut down trees. Stumps were burned or dynamited later. As Roy guided the plow, which sometimes jammed with roots and hurled him off his feet, Ray carried a hoe to kill poisonous snakes. Cotton seeds, planted in April, would grow by October into four-foot-high plants.

At the house, Carrie swatted flies buzzing by the thousands onto window screens and doors. She collected rain for drinking water; the well water, high in iron content, turned everything boiled in it green, and curdled soap into lumps. Carrie taught the children how to pour lime into a water-filled barrel so it could pull the iron to the bottom.

Johnny's first chores in Dyess were feeding chickens and carrying water into the hot fields to his father, brothers, and older sister. When he was big enough to drag a six-foot, and then a nine-foot, canvas sack filled with over thirty pounds of flourishing cotton, he worked the rows before and after school. By then, he had a new sister and brother: Joanne, born in 1938, and Tommy, in 1940.

Johnny, now ten and the quietest of the Cash children, played a game in the fields with seven-year-old Reba to keep their minds off the stinging hand cuts that came from prickly cotton bolls. Reba would recite a few words of a song from their mother's repertoire, and Johnny, whose memory astonished the family, would sing every word of every verse, even from songs he had heard only once.

The constant picking of cotton, however, made him restless. Once, he ran off the fields with a stick and broke dozens of jars in a neighbor's barn. Days later, when his mother questioned him, he didn't lie. Carrie had been taking him to the Baptist Church of God on Road Fifteen, and he knew about hell, fire, and damnation.

If the seven children weren't attending church, weeding, hoeing, picking, digging up potatoes, cutting and hauling hay, feeding farm animals, pouring lime into water barrels, or dragging canvas bags through cotton fields, they might steal a few hours from their chores to swim or fish at Blue Hole on the Tyronza River. Johnny sometimes hiked with his dog, Jake Terry, a stray his father let him keep. He and Jack taught the dog to retrieve sticks and to wait in the schoolyard, but when Jake Terry broke into the chicken coop and killed two chickens, Ray Cash dragged him into the woods and shot him with a .22 rifle. Johnny went looking everywhere for his dog until he found him dead, foam seeping from his mouth. "Why? Why?" he asked his father, but Ray's gruff reply about chewed-up chickens only made Johnny feel the harshness of farm life and of his father's strict authority.

He kept singing the gospel songs he learned—"Draw Me Nearer," "Amazing Grace," and "Life's Evening Sun Is Sinking Low," the one the family sang in the fields at twilight. He made a friend, eleven-year-old Jesse Barnhill, who played guitar and lived near Blue Hole. Infantile paralysis, or polio, had crippled Jesse's right leg and withered his right arm to half its normal length. Other children teased him as he hobbled to school, but he ignored them, strumming country music on an old Gibson flattop guitar. He sang songs by Hank Snow, Jimmie Rodgers, the Carter Family, and Ernest Tubb, all well-known country stars of the day.

Second to gospel, Johnny loved country music. Often labeled "hillbilly" by city people who preferred pop and classical music, country music had roots in early folk music (mournful songs of poor, white Southerners) and in reels and jigs (Irish tunes) brought to America by white settlers from the British Isles. Country's counterpart was the rhythmic, soulful music of Southern blacks: spirituals, ragtime, blues, and jazz. Barriers that many whites put up between themselves and blacks often cracked when it came to music. Country songs borrowed heavily from black songs. African slaves brought the banjo, which is used with the fiddle for most country music, to America, and Southern black singers most likely introduced guitar to Southern white singers.

One afternoon, Johnny sat in the grass at Jesse Barnhill's house, watching him play guitar. Jesse formed chords with his good left hand while his shrunken right hand beat out a pulsing rhythm. Johnny felt himself trembling at the stirring sounds.

"You've got infantile paralysis," he told his friend, "but you sure can play the guitar."

Jesse's answer would stay with Johnny for the rest of his life. "Sometimes," he said, "when you lose a gift, you get another one."

Walking home that night, Johnny's head was spinning at the memory of Jesse's songs. He wasn't wearing shoes (he saved them for school and church), and his toes ached on the gravel road. He'd left Jesse's house later than usual. Panthers or cottonmouth snakes might lunge at him out of the bushes, even kill him. So with nearly three miles to go past the night's scary shapes, he started singing, and he didn't stop. He sang every word of every song that Jesse had played.

"I sang through the dark," Johnny wrote about that solitary walk in Dyess and of his memories of Jesse Barnhill, "and decided that that kind of music was going to be my magic to take me through all the dark places."

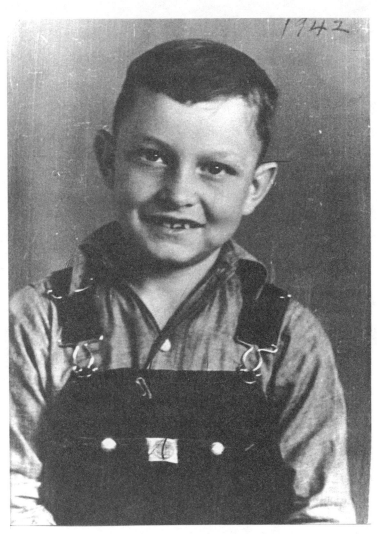

Johnny (age 10) in the fourth grade, 1942.

TWO

NEWS OF "GOINGS-ON" in Dyess—births, deaths, marriages, injuries, arrivals of new families, and, of course, crop yields—were passed along at church gatherings and the community store. On Fridays, news appeared in mimeographed copies of the *Colony Herald* newspaper. But Ray and Carrie Cash felt out of touch with happenings beyond Dyess, so after they saved a few extra dollars, they ordered a battery-operated table radio from the Sears Roebuck & Co. catalog. It was through this wooden box with its knobs and fabric-covered speaker that twelve-year-old Johnny discovered a whole universe of music.

At first, the radio was prized for its bulletins about a calamitous, twenty-one-day rainfall in Dyess. In 1937, the Mississippi River rose fifteen feet above flood level, and farmers feared that rain and winds would collapse river levees, letting floods destroy Dyess. When water rose above the Cashes' porch steps, Ray and Roy carried the chickens into the house, opened the food bin in the barn for the pig, and dragged the cow and mule through muddy waters to a holding barn in the center of Dyess. As families evacuated the colony, small bridges and dead animals floated everywhere. Ray and Roy decided to stay put in town, but Carrie and the younger children, including Johnny, left by bus and then train to Carrie's family in Kingsland.

Eventually winds shifted, and the levees miraculously held. After a month, the Cashes returned home. Wild dogs growled at them from the yard, and in the house they found mounds of mud and cow-itch vines on the floors, and eggs laid on the couch by the chickens. Ray had to beat snakes off the barn rafters. At the rear of the pigpen were five piglets born during the evacuation. Some families were not so fortunate. Houses were destroyed, and people contracted pneumonia.

The radio reported Dyess's slow but steady recovery. Rain had brought in good sediment from the riverbed; cotton crops were better than ever that year. In its own way, Dyess fulfilled its promise. Farmers received their share in profits, and doodlum was replaced by real money. Ray dismantled the squeaky cart on rusted iron wheels that he had used for hauling and bought himself a farm wagon.

One day, when he was older, Johnny would write a song, "Five Feet High and Rising," about the twenty-one-day rain in Dyess:

> How high is the water, Mama? Five feet high
>   and rising.
> How high is the water, Papa? She said five feet
>   high and rising.
>
> Well, the rails are washed out north of town;
> We gotta head for higher ground.
> We can't come back till the water goes down.
> Five feet high and rising . . .

Turning the knob back and forth on the Sears Roebuck radio, Johnny discovered high-frequency country-music stations broadcasting across the U.S. and into Canada from barn dances, rodeos, and state fairs. One station was located just over the Mexican border. The first radio song Johnny heard, "Hobo Bill's Last Ride" by Jimmie Rodgers, sent tingles through his ears. "[It was about] a man dying alone in a freezing boxcar," Johnny would say, mindful of how his father once rode the blinds of Old 90. "[It] felt so real, so close to home. . . ."

Soon he not only knew words to country songs but had memorized call letters and station locations. Sitting in the living room at what his mother called their library table, listening to the Grand Ole Opry on WSM or the Carter Family on XERF, Johnny gave more attention to the radio than to his homework. His school marks were Bs and Cs, with an occasional A in English or history, but his teachers said he was smart enough to earn all As. With the radio playing, he'd tap his feet on the floor or, out of excitement over the music, dig notches into the four-foot-long table with his pocketknife. His mother urged him to stop his "diggings," but he always forgot.

Working the cotton fields at lunchtime, he ran home between twelve thirty and one P.M. to hear WMPS's "High Noon Roundup" with Smilin' Eddie Hill and Ira and Charlie Louvin, the Louvin Brothers.

Somehow one P.M. would turn into one fifteen P.M. and, munching on a hunk of homemade cheese, knowing he would be reprimanded by his father, he would come late to the fields.

Carrie Cash was happy about her son's interest in music, but her husband scoffed at it. Radio music, Ray said, was "fake stuff" sung by people who weren't "really there." It wasn't like hymns at church, or songfests at home around the thirty-seven-dollar piano. Seeing Johnny at the radio, Ray worried that what he'd taught him—hard work, thrift, responsibility—would come to nothing. "You'll never do any good," Ray told Johnny, "as long as you've got that music on the mind."

Bedtime in the Cash house was 8:10 P.M., after Ray and Carrie listened to the evening news. By then, schoolwork left behind, Johnny was back at the radio, turning the knob. Most of his sisters and brothers were ready for bed, except for Jack. He stayed up with Johnny to read the Bible. Jack, husky and solid at fourteen, was the Dyess newspaper boy, loved by everyone who knew him. He carried his Bible to school, church, and even into the fields, confiding in his mother that he felt called to be a preacher like her Methodist grandfather, or like the four Baptist preachers from his father's family, successors to a Scottish lineage that brought mariner William Caesche to Virginia in 1673 as the first Caesche settler in America.

Ray Cash never spoke harshly to Jack; future preachers, he said, should be treated with kid gloves. But after eight thirty, when the radio was still spewing out music, Ray often lost patience with Johnny. He ordered him to turn off the radio and blow out the lamp. "You won't want to get up in the morning!" he'd yell. "Blow that light out!"

Waving good night to Jack, Johnny would edge closer to the table and turn the radio down, not off. An ear pressed against the speaker, he would keep listening to at least three or four more songs. As always, the music carried him to some imaginary place outside Dyess, away from the endless cycle of weeds, worms, and grinding work. He felt as if an engine buzzed inside him so he could barely keep still. But then his father's voice would bellow, *Turn that radio off!*

"Yes," Johnny would whisper, his feet continuing to tap softly on the floor. He'd do it—in the next minute. Really he would. He knew he should obey his father.

But first . . . just one more song. Okay? Just one more chorus. Okay? Just one more note.

The Church of God on Road Fifteen was one place where music, sung by a gospel choir, was never "fake." Johnny and Jack walked to church together; because of his brother, Johnny was learning Bible passages by heart. When he was six years old, he had felt fearful at church. The preacher would shout, moan, and pull people from the pews and tug them to the altar. "Come to God!" he would gasp. "Repent!" Women, and sometimes men, would fall, writhing, to the floor. "Hallelujah!" the preacher would shout. "Praise God! Praise God! Praise God!" Trembling, Johnny Cash "didn't understand it [all] as worship then."

God, Jack said to Johnny, would watch over his brother in ways Jack couldn't, and would forgive him for stealing some of their father's cigarette butts and smoking them in the outhouse. Johnny liked the tobacco taste and the glowing red tip of the cigarette, but he never liked disappointing Jack. "[No] two boys in a family," he'd say, "were ever closer to one another or loved each other more than me and my brother Jack."

Jack often told the story of Jesus Christ, who Jack said died for man's sins. But sinners could be redeemed, and bad things could become good things. So Johnny, at twelve years old, figured he would be sinning if he didn't accept Jesus—and he would be rejecting his brother. The songs he heard on the radio seemed to guide him somehow. One Sunday in early 1944, "twitchy and nervous," he vaulted out of his church seat and took the preacher's hand. He pledged his "spiritual accountability." Afterwards, on the walk home, he felt even closer to Jack. "I really had something in common with him," he'd say. "Jack and I could walk like this forever—children of God."

When school closed that May, the Cashes hauled hundred-pound bags of cotton seed to the fields. Several acres were put aside for corn, beans, tomatoes, strawberries, and sweet potatoes. Ray finally owned his property, a great source of pride for the family. He had been granted a $2,183.60 mortgage, a hefty sum for a poor farmer, but he could pay it off at $111.41 a year.

On a Saturday in early May, Johnny asked Jack to go fishing with him at Blue Hole, but Jack said no. He had agreed to cut fence posts at the school agricultural shop, and the family needed the three dollars he would earn. But Johnny didn't stop asking. As the brothers set off down the road, Jack said he felt strange about working that day. Waving his arms, he left Johnny at the spot dividing their two destinations, going on alone but imitating the voice of the cartoon character Bugs Bunny. "What's up, doc?" he yelled. Weaving under the trees, he started imitating Porky Pig, another character. Johnny had never seen his brother act that way.

After two hours at Blue Hole, Johnny felt uneasy. He pulled his pole out of the water and headed home. Suddenly he saw his father driving toward him full speed in the preacher's Model A Ford. Screeching to a stop, Ray Cash told his son to toss the fishing pole in a ditch and get in the car. Something awful, Ray said, had happened to Jack. He sounded angry that Johnny had gone fishing. Back at the house, he picked up a paper grocery sack and led him into the smokehouse.

Ray dumped the contents of the sack, Jack's clothes, onto the floor. Shirt, pants, and belt were slashed and blood-soaked. Ray, tears streaming down his face, said a saw handle had yanked Jack into its blade, ripping him open from ribs to groin. An ambulance took him to the hospital, but he had insisted on sitting up. He told the driver he was holding in his intestines. Other parts of him, he said, were chopped to bits, lying near the saw.

Doctors, having performed surgery, said Jack wouldn't live. Roy was called home from Memphis, where he worked now as a mechanic, and Louise, who was married, came from Osceola, Arkansas. Jack, however, was stronger than the doctors knew. By Wednesday, he was briefly smiling, talking, and reading mail from friends. The family attended church, offering special prayers, then returned to their vigil at Jack's bedside. Johnny, numb with grief, tried talking to his brother, but Jack seemed oddly unconcerned. Only later did Johnny realize that Jack must have known death was near. In saying so little, he seemed to be telling the "Shoo-Doo" he had always protected, "You're going to learn to live without me, so start learning now."

By Friday, Jack was ashen and clammy, lying with his eyes shut. The doctors were solemn. While the family formed a circle around the bed, Jack began mumbling incoherently. Weeping, Carrie wiped her son's forehead, but suddenly his eyes opened and he stared at her. He had seen such a beautiful river, he told her, stretching in two directions. And angels were singing. Oh, the singing! Could she hear?

"No, son, I can't. . . ." Carrie replied softly.

"I wish you could," Jack whispered. "They're so beautiful. . . ."

In the next moment, Jack's body stiffened and, as Johnny one day wrote, "He had intestinal poisoning, and that stuff came out of his mouth onto his chest, and he was gone."

On the day of the funeral, family and friends tried consoling one another. For Johnny, there was no consolation, "no way around grief and loss." He felt as if he, too, had died. A sermon was given at the Church of God, and Jack's casket was borne to a cemetery in the town of Bassett. Six Boy Scouts carried the casket to an open grave as Carrie and Ray led hymns in Jack's honor: "Peace in the Valley," "Shall We Gather at the River?" "I'll Fly Away." Johnny's voice, still pitched at a childhood tenor, rose toward the sky:

> *When the shadows of this life have flown,*
> *I'll fly away.*
> *Like a bird from prison bars has flown,*
> *I'll fly away.*

I'll fly away, O Glory,
  I'll fly away.
When I die, Hallelujah, bye and bye,
  I'll fly away.

On a simple granite headstone at Jack's grave was carved JACK D. CASH 1929–1944. Above the name was a question that Johnny would carry like the Holy Grail: WILL YOU MEET ME IN HEAVEN? He would always wonder how he could have kept Jack from cutting fence posts on the day of the accident. Love and admiration for his brother would be woven into the tapestry of many Johnny Cash songs. And throughout his life, when Johnny lost his way, he would ask two questions of his own: "Which is Jack's way? Which direction would *he* have taken?"

THREE

ON THE MONDAY after Jack's funeral, Dyess families awoke to their usual chores. Cows had to be milked, chickens fed. Farmers greased their rifles, waitresses set the café tables. From his front porch, Johnny looked for some sign that the world wasn't the same. How had the sun come up? Why had the watermelons grown fatter? How could the day just be ordinary?

Over the following weeks, he had a hard time going to the fields. His mother was digging weeds, kneeling in the dirt with a tear-stained face. His father, grim and bereft, hauled seed and supplies from the store. Even four-year-old Tommy, filling the water pail, seemed sad. *Stop!* Johnny wanted to shout. *Can't you stop?*

Before Jack's accident, Johnny had brought home a slab of sandstone that he left on the porch. Colony land was plowed so flat and rock-free that the eye could see thirty miles ahead. Naming the slab "Hoxie

Rock," Johnny had sat with his feet on it, gazing at the horizon and listening through an open window to WMPS-Memphis on the radio. But, missing Jack now, he twisted into himself, leaving Hoxie Rock stranded, and wrote poems—or maybe they were songs.

Family and friends found him especially quiet, withdrawn. As summer heat browned thickets of cottonwood and willow trees, he swam by himself at Blue Hole. He had five teenage friends who said they were sorry about his brother, but that he shouldn't ignore his pals. Finally, by August, he joined them. They always pooled whatever money they could scrape together for Saturday-night movies at the colony center. One Saturday, a boy named Paul East had eight dollars from chopping cotton but refused to divvy up. At last, some of Johnny's anger and grief had a place to go. He knocked Paul to the ground, sat on his stomach, and took the money.

By the time Johnny was in Dyess High School, he had sung a few solos at church and won five dollars in a school contest singing "That Lucky Old Sun." His voice hadn't dropped yet, surprising his mother since her father sang baritone from his early teens. Then, after a day of working a crosscut saw for six hours, Johnny trudged home for supper, unconsciously singing a gospel tune. Carrie dropped the kettle when she heard him, blurting out, "Who was that singing in such a low, booming voice?"

"That was me," Johnny answered, realizing what had happened.

Exploring his new range, he sang again, showing his mother how deep he could go. "God has His hand on you, son," Carrie said. "Don't ever forget the gift."

Could a gift at song, if he had it, ever put him on radio, Johnny wondered? Like the Louvin Brothers? Pipe dreams, his father warned. But his mother soon gave him a $6.98 Sears Roebuck guitar. Johnny felt strange with it, however, and laid it by Jack's Bible. Wanting him to have voice lessons, Carrie took in washing and ironing, and arranged to send him, at fifty cents a half hour, to Miss LaVanda Mae Fiedler.

At his first lesson, Miss Fiedler asked Johnny to sing something, so he did Hank Williams's country hit, "Long Gone Lonesome Blues." At Miss Fiedler's request, he sang it a second time. That's when she said she couldn't teach him anything, and not to change his style. He was a natural, she told him. Johnny was glad his mother could stop doing other people's laundry.

At school, Johnny had a crush on Virginia North, who dated a boy from Osceola. He wrote her notes but felt too shy to deliver them. Then his father bought the family's first car, an old Ford with no heater. Its windows had broken on the rutted roads and were filled in with cardboard.

One afternoon Johnny drove the car to the Dyess café, wheels whipping up gravel onto the rusty bumper. When he saw Virginia North, he thought she might ride with him. He slammed on the brakes, but they didn't hold, and the car knocked against the porch. The cardboard popped out of the windows.

For some reason, Virginia smiled, so Johnny asked her to go to the movies. He'd have to get real windows, she replied flatly, before she'd ever be seen with him.

Driving home, Johnny decided someday he would have a car with windows. Would Virginia North still be picking cotton in Dyess? In his new, low voice, he began singing "Candy Kisses," a song that played on the jukebox at the café.

Johnny, like Jack, had grown muscular in his teens. He could pick close to 350 pounds of cotton a day. He joined the 4-H Club and the Boy Scouts and was such a strong swimmer, he crossed the Mississippi

River. He even won an Arkansas boys' state swimming championship.

Because of President Roosevelt's resettlement colonies and work projects (WPAs), the poverty of the Depression years had decreased, but at harvest time the colony still teemed with starving migrants pleading for work. In 1948, Johnny was hired along with migrants and farmers to clear brush at the Tyronza River. He ran forty-pound cans of water to the thirsty crew. He did not last long at the job. Jumping into Dyess workers' cars, he flipped on the radios. The music kept him from his loneliness over Jack, but when his listening made someone's car battery die, he was fired.

In spring of that year, he had tuned in to *High Noon Roundup* on WMPS and almost couldn't believe his ears. Smilin' Eddie Hill announced that Charlie and Ira Louvin, the tenor duo, would perform at Dyess High School. Johnny couldn't stop talking about it. The Louvins were born in Alabama, where they'd labored in cotton mills and sung gospel, folk, and country. The night of the show, Johnny ran to school two hours early.

A long black limousine, a sight never seen in Dyess, finally pulled up to the doors. Seven people unloaded

musical instruments, a sound system, and boxes of souvenirs. Ira Louvin, whom Johnny recognized from newspaper photos, carried a mandolin into the school, but Charlie headed right for Johnny, asking for directions to the restroom. Trying to breathe, Johnny escorted him there, then to the auditorium. He was inches away from the famous tenor; he could touch his sleeve!

As he walked, Charlie Louvin ate soda crackers out of his pocket. "Are they good for your throat?" Johnny asked nervously. Whatever Charlie answered, he couldn't have known that the starstruck young fellow at his side would, for years to come, never turn down a chance to eat soda crackers.

Most of Dyess had turned up for the show. The Louvin Brothers joked and sang hymns and gospel songs. Sitting in the auditorium's front row, Johnny was thrilled. Two hours seemed to him like twenty minutes. After the last song, the audience clapped until the air vibrated, and Johnny hurried outside. Ira and Charlie, their foreheads glistening in the single school light, were soon reloading the limousine, then signing autographs and selling souvenirs. Johnny couldn't bring himself to ask for signatures, and he had

no money for trinkets. Instead, he stood at attention in the shadows, wishing Jack were beside him.

The limousine took off like one of the black panthers he'd been told about from the Arkansas hills, heading down Road One toward the Memphis highway. Johnny managed a wave, and wonder of wonders, Charlie Louvin waved back. "He remembered me!" Johnny would write of the evening. He stayed motionless by the door light, a lone figure hanging on to what his father had called "pipe dreams." In his mind he saw an auditorium stage. He saw spotlights and a microphone, a singer and an audience. Suddenly he had no doubts. "I'll be up there someday," he whispered, his heart thudding. "That's what I'm gonna be."

In 1950, Johnny graduated from Dyess High School. No longer as quiet, he had developed an edgy boldness. Next to his photo in the school yearbook, the caption said: "Be a live wire and you won't get stepped on."

Though Ray Cash had rented out his land in 1949, having been appointed foreman at an oleomargarine factory in nearby Evadale, Johnny knew there wasn't money for college. He took a three-day job picking strawberries in west Arkansas for three dollars, then

hitchhiked home. Some of his friends were going "up North" for steady pay in Michigan automobile factories. Since he had no idea how to earn a living singing, he went with them.

Dewey Cox, the Dyess mailman, drove everyone to Wilson to board a train to Memphis and then a Greyhound bus to Detroit. Nearly broke, Johnny found cheap lodging in a Detroit boardinghouse. He hitchhiked twenty-five miles to the Fisher Body plant in Pontiac and applied for a job. "You're not gonna be like the other young guys from the South . . . are you?" the supervisor asked. "[They] work a couple of weeks or maybe a month, and they go home to Mama."

No, Johnny said, he'd stick around. But after several weeks of the monotony of lifting car hoods onto a punch press, he wasn't sure. He was used to the farm; it seemed like heaven compared to the auto plant. "Up North" was a foreign country to him. City boys at the plant called him *hick* or *hillbilly*, and in the long walks to work, he lost ten pounds. When he cut his right arm on a car hood, he quit, not caring what the supervisor thought. He hitchhiked back to Dyess, but he didn't come home poor. He had $150 in his pocket.

In early July, Johnny went the other route of many

young Southern men hungry for work. He drove his father's windowless Ford to the town of Blytheville and, with the Korean War barely three weeks old, enlisted in the United States Air Force. Ray Cash, being a war veteran, was proud. Johnny was dispatched for basic training to Lackland Air Force Base in Texas. The initials that were his birth name, J.R., weren't enough identification for the military; he was sworn in as "John Ray."

Four years in the air force, even with Johnny's sorrow over Jack like a lost arm or leg, would mold him into a tougher, rougher, six-foot-one-and-a-half-inch John Cash. After basic training, he chose the specialty of radio operator and learned Morse code so fast, he finished his course far ahead of other servicemen.

Johnny's instructors, impressed by his coding, signed him up for the USAF Security Service. He trained at Brooks, Texas, in the radio operation that could intercept international broadcasts. He held his own in a class of college graduates. "I was proud of the work I was doing," he would say, "because I excelled in it."

The U.S. and the Soviet Union had been waging a political Cold War between Democracy and Communism since the 1940s. Johnny tuned in to Soviet

Morse code broadcasts on a six-band receiver, distinguished what would be important to decoding analysts, and then tapped that out into Morse code. He gained a reputation for being able to cut through radio static. In September 1951, he was assigned to Security Service duty in Landsberg, West Germany. Before flying overseas, he took a short pass from Brooks to San Antonio. He went roller-skating at St. Mary's Rink, where he skidded one night into a pretty seventeen-year-old high school senior named Vivian Liberto. They began dating, and after three weeks, they were an "item." The Libertos were Catholic, not Baptist, but that didn't bother Johnny. They told him they loved music.

In Landsberg, missing Vivian, he spent grueling eight-hour shifts at a radio transmitter. In the barracks, he made five friends from the South who played country music on guitars, banjos, or mandolins. One of them taught him his first guitar chords, and to play rhythm with his thumb, his future signature style. He bought himself a guitar for only twenty Deutsche Marks (five U.S. dollars) and carried it to the barracks in knee-deep snow. He wrote Vivian that he looked like a snowman when he entered the gate.

The radio transmitter was strong enough to locate WSM in Nashville, and the "down-home boys" often listened to the Grand Ole Opry on Saturday nights. They formed their own music group, the Landsberg Barbarians, lugging their instruments when they took military leave to taverns and beer halls.

In letters home and to Vivian, Johnny never disclosed how, even though he had a Bible in Landsberg, he wasn't reading it much, or how he had finally given in to temptation and drunk his first German beer, or how he jumped into the scramble of sweaty tavern brawls. His nose was broken in a scuffle, and he had a small face scar from a cyst that was removed by a drunken doctor.

He knew he was ignoring what he'd been taught in Dyess about "the right way and the wrong way." One night, revved up and suddenly anxious, he recklessly threw a typewriter through a window and went to the dispensary for aspirin. Yet his superiors admired him, and he was appointed chief of the forty men on his shifts. He wrote a science-fiction story that would later be published, and he composed several songs— "Belshazzar," based on the ancient Babylonian king, whose story in the Bible Jack had known by heart, and "Hey, Porter," a country song printed in *Stars and Stripes*, the servicemen's magazine:

> *Hey, porter. Hey, porter!*
> *Would you tell me the time?*
> *How much longer will it be*
> *'Til we cross that Mason-Dixon Line? . . .*

> *When we hit Dixie will you tell that engineer to ring*
>   *his bell,*
> *And ask everybody that ain't asleep to stand right up*
>   *and yell.*
> *Hey, porter. Hey, porter!*
> *It's getting light outside.*
> *This old train is puffin' smoke and I have to strain*
>   *my eyes.*
> *But ask that engineer if he will blow his whistle*
>   *please,*
> *'Cause I smell frost on cotton leaves,*
> *And I smell that Southern breeze. . . .*

> *Hey, porter. Hey, porter!*
> *Please open up my door.*
> *When they stop this train I'm gonna get off first*

'Cause I can't wait no more.
Tell that engineer I say, "Thanks a lot, and I didn't
*   mind the fare.*
I'm gonna set my feet on Southern soil
And breathe that Southern air.

Before Johnny's air force stint ended on July 3, 1954, he had what he would call his "only real [military] fight." He took a carton of cigarettes to the front gate of the base, planning to sell it in town. Two security

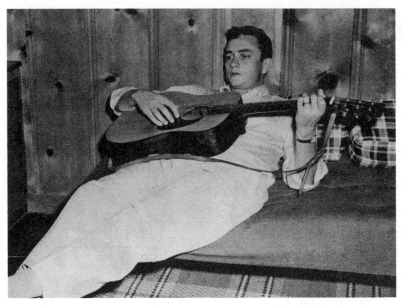

Johnny strumming his guitar after his return home from the air force.

guards stopped him and grabbed the cigarettes for themselves. Outraged, Johnny lured the men past the gate and off military property. He knocked them both down a fifty-foot embankment. One man lost teeth, and the other broke his nose.

As the guards ran off, Johnny stood on the rim of the embankment. He knew his Dyess minister would have admonished him to "Repent! Seek forgiveness for your sins!" And in truth, he did believe in the redeeming, forgiving grace of God. But sometimes the wrong way seemed to strong-arm the right way. It would be good, he told himself, to be a civilian again, to see Vivian and his family, to return to the South of his "Hey, Porter" song.

He could once more listen to WLW in New Orleans and WMPS in Memphis. He and Jesse Barnhill could sing up a storm. And, taking a cue from Charlie Louvin, he just might buy himself a big box of soda crackers. John Cash, Air Force Staff Sergeant, now able to play guitar while he sang, was coming home.

FOUR

IN A PHONE CALL from West Germany, twenty-two-year-old Johnny asked Vivian Liberto to marry him, and she agreed. Except for their letters, they hardly knew each other. They had been ice-skating and to the movies, and Johnny had eaten a few of Mrs. Liberto's Italian dinners before he went overseas, but separation and wartime romance had prompted their talk of "forever after." Discharged at Camp Kilmer, New Jersey, Johnny flew to Tennessee to find Vivian waiting for him with his parents, brothers, and sisters.

They were married at St. Ann's Church in San Antonio on August 7, 1954. The priest conducting the ceremony was Vivian's uncle, and Roy Cash was best man. The day was hot, and Johnny, who couldn't afford a suit, sweated in his air force dress uniform. After a short reception at St. Anthony Hotel, the newlyweds

bid good-bye to their families. Piling into Roy's car, they drove through the Ozark Mountains to the tiny walk-up flat they had rented in Memphis.

Though Vivian encouraged her new husband's singing, she knew even less than he did about surviving on it. So when Roy told Johnny that the Home Equipment Company on Summer Avenue needed a salesman, he got himself hired. He also signed up under the G.I. Bill for a radio announcer course at Keegan's School of Broadcasting. He wasn't about to lose his dreams to selling refrigerators, vacuums, and washing machines.

It was Johnny's honesty, even bluntness, that made him low man on the totem pole at Home Equipment Company. Going door to door in the poorest sections of Memphis, he was supposed to sell used machines. But he hated talking people into buying what they couldn't afford. Once, he stopped a woman from purchasing an overpriced secondhand refrigerator.

Housewives invited Johnny into their dingy houses to look at upright vacuum cleaners with zippered bags. Reluctantly, he would begin his demonstration. Now and then, however, he'd see a guitar leaning against

a wall, and he would grab it up and stop his sales pitch in mid-sentence. Sitting on the edge of a chair, he would strum and sing for a half hour or more. The housewife might clap her hands or call in her kids to listen. But if she didn't remind him about the vacuum, it would lie flat on the floor like a discarded piece of junk.

His commissions at Home Equipment Company hardly paid for living expenses, and after managing a down payment on a 1954 Plymouth, he didn't have money to take Vivian, who was pregnant now and homesick, to see her family. Looking out for his brother, Roy gave him fifty dollars.

Memphis, like Nashville, was a city of music. The blues—a style combining African tribal rhythms and harmonies with American church music—were born there. Along Beale Street, the blues shared space with soul, rhythm-and-blues, jazz, gospel, folk, country, and, beginning in the 1950s, rock 'n' roll. Musicians played the smoky nightclubs, juke joints, and honky-tonks. Seedy characters crowded liquor stores and pawnshops. A man was said to have jumped out of a taxicab on Beale Street, looking to pawn his artificial leg.

Johnny knew that as much as he hated his job, he couldn't quit this time. He had a pregnant wife and bills to pay, and he worried over Vivian climbing the steep stairs to their walk-up apartment. When he rented another apartment, one with fewer stairs, he persuaded the landlady, Pat Isom, to wait for the fifty-five-dollar rent. Mrs. Isom didn't know that the polite and handsome young man would usually be late paying rent, or that he spent some of the meager cash in his pocket on records like *Blues in the Mississippi Night,* his favorite album of Delta songs.

On his Home Equipment route, Johnny covered Orange Mound, the Memphis ghetto, where he met Gus Cannon, an old and grizzled black handyman who wrote songs and played a five-string banjo. Sitting with Gus on his porch, stunned by the sounds the handyman's fingers coaxed from the banjo, Johnny arranged his route to end each workday in Orange Mound. He never tried to sell Gus anything. And he was glad when, eight years later, Gus's song "Walk Right In" became a hit single with the Rooftop Singers.

Besides getting married, the biggest thing that

happened to Johnny in 1954 was meeting two Memphis auto mechanics, Luther Perkins and Marshall Grant. Both men worked with Roy at Automobile Sales Company, but if they didn't have work to do, they played guitar in the washroom. Marshall, who had been the North Carolina champion cotton picker, played bass guitar; Luther, son of a Baptist minister in Mississippi, loved gospel music. After hours, while their wives played cards, they jammed in each other's houses.

At Roy's suggestion, Johnny showed up at the garage. "I saw him coming down the rows of cars," Marshall would say. "There was something that caught your attention. He was tall and dark, and he was as edgy as a cat on a tin roof." It didn't take long before the three men were meeting regularly at Luther's house. Johnny brought his guitar and, on the first night, played and sang Hank Snow's "Moving On." Luther and Marshall accompanied him. Since the neighbors didn't complain, gospel and country songs continued until dawn.

Before long, picking and strumming together, the trio decided to name themselves. Johnny thought

"The Tennessee Three" looked good with its three
Ts and Southern flavor, but Luther and Marshall
graciously suggested "John Cash and the Tennessee
Two." Johnny stayed with his five-dollar German
guitar, Luther borrowed an electric Fender guitar, and
Marshall bought a secondhand stand-up bass. None
of them had professional training, but they created a
unique, if raw, sound. Cautious on his Fender, Luther
played one note at a time and, for smoothness, removed
the guitar's metal plate so he could muffle the strings
with his right palm. Johnny stuck small bits of paper
through his strings, creating a rhythmic, rattling effect
like brushes on a snare drum.

When fall leaves finished layering Beale Street and
Gus Cannon's porch, and Vivian Cash was in her
fourth month of pregnancy, Johnny was, as usual, broke.
He and his two cohorts couldn't tune their stand-up
bass because they didn't know its note positions but,
laughing and scratching their heads, they used a guitar
to identify the notes, then marked them on the bass
with tape. So there they were just before winter, this
hodgepodge trio with no training, no show-business
savvy, one cheap guitar, one borrowed guitar, and one

secondhand, taped-up bass. They were an unlikely bet, a shot in the dark.

When the trio jammed, the yard at Luther's house filled with neighbors. The three young men struck up a harmony, leaping into tunes from the mountains of Alabama and Tennessee, hushing into blues or gospel from churches, revival meetings, old slave ships, or prison chain gangs. And there was Johnny's voice— deep, strong, lonesome, lifting like an eagle above the guitars.

One neighbor asked the trio to perform at a church in North Memphis. Luther bought a worn-down amplifier, and the three of them decided to dress alike. Since they didn't own suits or ties, black shirts became the band outfit, and for Johnny the black just felt right. A few weeks later, they played for free at Bob's Barbecue on Summer Avenue, raising funds for a friend of Marshall's who had been hurt in a motorboat accident. The crowd really applauded Johnny's "Belshazzar"; it dug deeper than the fluff songs on jukeboxes.

Another gig offer came from George Bates, Johnny's boss at Home Equipment Company. George had long

gone the extra mile for his reluctant salesman, even loaning him money. Hearing that Johnny wanted to sing, he paid radio station KWEM-Memphis fifteen dollars per week to feature the trio for eight weeks of fifteen-minute segments on Saturday afternoons. Johnny, who had been regularly attending Baptist church again while Vivian went to Catholic Mass, would sing gospel. Helped by his broadcasting class at Keegan's, he plugged Home Equipment Company for George Bates. Remembering the Sears Roebuck radio in Dyess, he wanted to grin. Now his voice would be on it. He longed to tell Jack. As it was, Vivian, Roy, and Roy's wife, Wandene, cheered him on.

Taking Vivian with him in the Plymouth, Johnny drove to nearby towns, many of which contained more bars than stoplights. He hunted for bookings at outdoor arenas, barn dances, schools, or movie theater intermissions. His first success was at Hurst Motor Company in Memphis, which hired the trio for an afternoon. Riding up and down streets on a flatbed truck, Johnny, Luther, and Marshall played and sang their hearts out. They split the fifty-dollar payment three ways.

Sun Studio, the famous recording studio in Memphis, Tennessee, where artists including Elvis Presley, Johnny Cash, Roy Orbison, and Jerry Lee Lewis made albums.

Dreaming of cutting a gospel record, Johnny paged through a list of music producers and settled on Sam Phillips of Sun Studio, a thirty-two-year-old hotshot who, Johnny said later in admiration, "didn't run with the pack." Although Phillips's business had thrived on black artists like B.B. King, Little Milton, and Howlin' Wolf, he had broken the unwritten, racist rule in the South that a studio could record either black or white musicians, not both. In fact, he had signed a young white trucker named Elvis Presley whose single, "That's

All Right, Mama," was "tearing up the airways" and launching, with electric guitar, the new, hip-swinging rock 'n' roll.

Johnny's nerve soon overcame his shyness. He telephoned Sam Phillips, saying he was a singer with a gospel background. Would Mr. Phillips be willing to see him? The answer was a polite but firm "No." Gospel records, Sam Phillips said, hardly made a profit. He couldn't take a chance on them. He wished Johnny good luck.

One week later, Johnny phoned again. This time he talked to Sam Phillips's receptionist, saying he sang country music. Could he make an appointment with Mr. Phillips? The receptionist hemmed and hawed, giving excuses before she hung up. Mr. Phillips was busy. He was out of town.

Finally, early enough in the morning that stores and offices hadn't opened yet, Johnny went to Sun Records. He sat on the curb, waiting for Sam Phillips. When he arrived, Johnny jumped to his feet and introduced himself. "Mr. Phillips, sir," he added, "if you listen to me, you'll be glad you did."

It was the right thing to say. Impressed by Johnny's

confidence, Sam Phillips invited him inside. A microphone, with a nearby amplifier, was on a metal stand. Johnny explained that he had two backup guitarists performing with him on KWEM radio, then after a gulp began singing alone. He sang Jimmie Rodgers songs, Hank Snow songs, Carter Family songs. He sang country songs he'd memorized from the radio and sung in the cotton fields. When Sam Phillips asked if he'd written any songs, he sang "Belshazzar" and several others from his air force days. "Anything else?" Sam Phillips asked. Hesitant, not sure if it was good enough, Johnny sang "Hey, Porter." Sam Phillips nodded. "Come back tomorrow with those guys you've been making the music with," he said, "and we'll put that song down."

John Cash and the Tennessee Two walked into Sun Records accompanied by A. W. "Red" Kernodle, a mechanic who played steel guitar at Luther's house. Johnny and Marshall were hell-bent on doing their best. Luther, however, was quaking in his scuffed shoes, and Red—who'd come along for added punch—was in a cold sweat. Sitting in the waiting room, trying to tune his guitar, he panicked. Telling his

friends he was too nervous, he fled out the door.

The first track recorded by the trio was "Wide Open Road," which, Johnny would say, "sounded awful." So did the next four songs. Then "Folsom Prison Blues," one of Johnny's air force pieces, finally jelled. Though the trio's untrained playing was rough, the vibrating out of Luther's unusual string muting and Marshall's growling bass created a rhythmic *boom-chicka-boom* sound that Sam Phillips had never heard.

Johnny had written "Folsom Prison Blues" after seeing a film about the California prison. He borrowed part of the melody from a 1953 song by composer Gordon Jenkins. Yet unlike most country-music prison lyrics, the convict in Johnny's story line, a lifer for murder, doesn't express regret or claim innocence. He hates prison, but admits he "had it coming":

> *I hear that train a-comin',*
> *It's rolling around the bend.*
> *And I ain't seen the sunshine*
> *Since I don't know when.*
> *I'm stuck in Folsom prison,*

And time keeps draggin' on.
But that train keeps a-rollin'
On down to San Antone. . . .

Impressed by the starkness of "Folsom Prison Blues," Sam Phillips decided John Cash—Phillips was the one to persuade him to use the name "Johnny" to attract teenage crowds—was a singer/songwriter of grit and power. The producer was particularly struck by two lines in the prison song that became Johnny Cash's most famous:

But I shot a man in Reno,
Just to watch him die.

When asked about those lines, Johnny said he'd tried to think of the worst possible reason a man might have for killing someone.

At the end of the recording session, Sam Phillips told the exhausted trio that he would put them on a future record. He chose "Hey, Porter" for one side of the first release and asked Johnny to write a teenage "weeper," or sad ballad, for the other. As country-music

critic and author Stephen Miller wrote: "A star, and a sound with which he would be forever associated, had been born and it had all been done on a shoestring in a studio not much bigger than the living room of an average house."

Johnny hurried from Sun Records toward the apartment on Tutwiler Avenue, where Vivian and their soon-to-be-born child waited. Baby clothes, diapers, and a crib needed to be bought. Hospital bills would arrive. Out of the goodness of her heart, the landlady had just paid their overdue electric bill. Reaching into his pocket, Johnny found only fifteen cents. Well, if a record of "Hey, Porter" was successful enough for the country charts, it might help pay the bills. Disk jockeys might play it; bookings might pour in. "Hey, Porter," backed by the weeper Johnny had promised Sam Phillips, might sell on Beale Street alongside the Louvin Brothers and even that new kid, Elvis Presley.

From the curb, a beggar in tattered clothes reached out a hand. Johnny stopped, slowly nodded, then dug back in his pocket. The fifteen cents he pressed into the beggar's palm on that afternoon in 1955 was a gift

far more generous than it seemed. Once more, Johnny was out of money, but he knew the beggar might be far worse off. With his five-dollar guitar slung over his shoulder, with Jack's spirit and his family nearby, and with Sam Phillips's "We're going to put out a record" ringing in his ears, Johnny Cash must have been counting his blessings.

FIVE

ON MAY 24, 1955, Johnny and Vivian Cash became parents. Little Rosanne, wailing in her mother's arms, would one day sing and write her own songs. When she came home to the apartment in Memphis, she was serenaded by guitar lullabies. Exactly one month later, on June 24, the new parents held not only their baby but Johnny's first record. The B-side was, as promised, "Hey, Porter." The A-side was "Cry, Cry, Cry," the weeper Johnny had written. It told of a woman whose wicked ways would lead her to heartbreak:

> *Everybody knows where you go when the sun goes down.*
> *I think you only live to see the lights of town.*
> *I wasted my time when I would try, try, try.*

Pausing during a studio session, circa 1960.

*When the lights have lost their glow, you're gonna
cry, cry, cry.*

Johnny dashed over to radio station WMPS-
Memphis with the 78-rpm record. Bob Neal, the disk
jockey, played one side while Johnny proudly watched
the yellow Sun label spin around on the turntable. But
in turning the record over, Neal accidentally broke it.
Hours later, Johnny realized how "green" he was about
the record business. He had thought the only copy of
his double release was gone, but Sam Phillips assured
him that boxes of "Cry, Cry, Cry/Hey, Porter" sat in
the storefront studio.

On his way home, Johnny heard "Hey, Porter"
on KCIJ-Shreveport, Louisiana. "I couldn't believe
it," he'd say. "All the way from Shreveport. This
was the miracle of the ages . . . 350 miles." His first
public appearance with Luther and Marshall after the
record release was as guest artist for Sonny James, a
popular country-music star, at a converted armory
in Covington, Tennessee. The trio's two songs, plus
some of Johnny's gospel music, delighted the audience.
"Cry, Cry, Cry" made both the Memphis and national
country charts, and sold over 100,000 copies in the

South. However, production costs at Sun Records ate a big chunk out of profits.

At night, while Vivian and Rosanne slept, Johnny wrote more songs. Sometimes blowing off his route for Home Equipment, he would fish for bookings in clubs like Tootsies Orchid Lounge or Pearl's Howdy Club. Driving to Bartlett and Germantown in Tennessee, or Newport and Forest City in nearby Arkansas, he'd tell club owners about his hit record on the Sun label. Nailing down a few bookings, he arranged with Luther and Marshall to tie the bass on top of the Plymouth and pile the guitars inside. The two mechanics were having a blast, but neither wanted to permanently leave their jobs. It was Johnny who plunged into showbiz, dragging his two friends along, putting over ninety thousand miles on the Plymouth in the next eighteen months. When valves burned out, Luther and Marshall sneaked the car into the Automobile Sales garage and fixed it.

Since signing Johnny, Sam Phillips had hired three new recording artists: Carl Perkins, a sharecropper's son whose boyhood guitar was a cigar box and a broom; Roy Orbison, another rock 'n' roll pioneer, whose trademark sunglasses covered bad eyesight;

and Jerry Lee Lewis, the rompin,' stompin' Bible lover who paid for his trip to Sun Records by selling thirty-three dozen eggs to neighbors. One afternoon at Sun Records, Johnny, Carl, Jerry Lee, and Elvis all happened to turn up at the same time. Gathering at the piano, the four began harmonizing on rock and gospel songs. The music and camaraderie were so boisterous, a studio engineer, Jack Clement, taped the impromptu session. Sam Phillips tipped off a newspaper reporter that Sun studio was "rockin'," and several reporters and music critics converged on the scene. A now-famous photograph of the four singers was taken, later captioned "The Million Dollar Quartet." Possessively, Jack Clement kept his tapes in a nearby bank vault for years before issuing them.

Johnny, Carl, and Roy quickly formed a close friendship. At a gig in Amory, Mississippi, Johnny told Carl about C. V. White, an air-force staff sergeant who'd been obsessed about clean clothes. "How do I look, man?" he'd ask Johnny before going on passes.

"Mighty spiffy," Johnny would say.

Though C.V. was wearing regulation air-force shoes, he'd joke: "Just don't step on my blue suede shoes."

Hearing the story, Carl grabbed a pencil and a brown paper bag. In ten minutes, he wrote the song "Blue Suede Shoes." Released by Sun, with Carl singing and playing guitar, it was a hit. Then Elvis recorded "Blue Suede Shoes," and it became an Elvis Presley classic.

Johnny's first Sun royalty check was for only $2.41. More money, however, was on the horizon. In August 1954, he, Luther, and Marshall played their first major concert, at Overton Park Shell in Memphis, headlining with Elvis and Sonny James. With Sam Phillips's help, they became part of a country-music troupe organized by disk jockey Bob Neal. The trio raced from Memphis to Tupelo, Mississippi, then sped to gigs in Lubbock, Brownwood, Amarillo, and San Angelo, Texas. They made the trip in Johnny's green, mud-caked Plymouth, which looked like a poor cousin to Elvis's flashy pink Cadillac, a gift from Sam Phillips.

Johnny's parents and siblings came to some of his bookings and sat in awe in the front row beneath stage lights. They heard what music reviewers, journalists, and cheering fans heard—the showstopping voice, the "sparse, no-frills" sound that was so intense that rafters shuddered. Johnny's songs told serious stories, unlike the simple or sugary themes of most country music. He didn't wear spangles or cowboy hats, nor did he drawl. He wore black; he stood onstage like he lived there, and if he wasn't always exactly in tune, it didn't matter.

"Even at age twenty-three," music critic Mikal Gilmore would say, "[his voice] conveyed a sense of haunted experience and regret with rare credibility." Perhaps the clearest account of Johnny's singing, given by a female fan, was quoted by editorial writer Tom Dearmore: "He just melts you down."

By year's end, the trio was booked on two of the South's biggest music shows, Louisiana Hayride and Big D Jamboree, both broadcast weekly on the radio. Only Nashville's Grand Ole Opry had more clout. Louisiana Hayride, based in Shreveport, hired Johnny to appear every Saturday night. Though travel expenses slashed into the trio's profits, Johnny saw that he just might make a living singing. So he didn't mind driving the seven hundred miles back and forth to Shreveport. If the landlady could babysit for Rosanne, Vivian came along. She got nervous, however, watching teenage girls howling, screaming, and fainting over Elvis. Would they do that with her husband? Would he be true to her?

For Johnny, road life was a maze of rigors and delights. Tight routine had shaped his years in Dyess. Now a roller coaster of roads, restaurants, and neon lights looped north to Iowa, south to Alabama and Louisiana, west to Texas, Colorado, and Arizona. The trio's pay rose to one hundred dollars per performance, but the not-so-trusty Plymouth guzzled gas and oil. When the wives stayed home, Johnny, Luther, and Marshall slept in four-dollar-a-night motels, smuggling in hot plates and a portable grill, eating pork chops or eggs with their hands. Exhausted from miles of road grind, they took turns between one lumpy bed and the floor.

They brought shotguns along in case their stomachs growled with hunger on the road and live "fixins"— rabbits, raccoons, ducks—were visible. According to writer Garth Campbell, if a "likely target appeared, whoever was driving would hit the brakes and skid the car to a stop, doors would fly open and they'd all scramble out, shooting in every direction."

Much as he loved the singing and adventure, Johnny missed Vivian and Rosanne. He was often so tired he didn't know up from down. How to tell one motel from another, one road from the one left behind?

At a stopover in Davenport, Iowa, cramped in an overheated motel room, he threw open the windows. By morning, a tiny mouse lay half-frozen on the sticky floor. After Marshall turned on the radiator so steam chugged out, Johnny lifted the mouse by its tail and held it cautiously over the heat. The little rodent had probably come through a hole, seeking shelter and warmth. When it squeaked and fluttered, Johnny—sometimes looking for refuge himself—ripped off part of a cloth and folded it into a square. As he left the motel room with his friends, slamming the door behind him, the gray mouse was safe on its makeshift pad atop the sputtering radiator.

Noting the success of "Hey, Porter" and "Cry, Cry, Cry," Sam Phillips released two more Johnny Cash singles: "So Doggone Lonesome" and his stark convict song from the air force, "Folsom Prison Blues." Both stayed on the country charts for twenty weeks. In another Sun release, "Train of Love," Johnny showed a developing ease in writing both internal and end rhymes:

Now train of love's a-leavin'
Leavin' my heart grievin',
But early or late, I sit and wait
Because I'm still believin'
We'll walk away together,
Though I may wait forever.

Sam Phillips added only a backup echo to guitars and bass on the new releases, creating an even more lonesome sound, letting Johnny's voice dominate rather than sink into the Nashville style of heavy orchestration.

Putting his trust in his singing, and paying back his old loans from George Bates, Johnny finally quit Home Equipment Company. And Luther and Marshall gave in on leaving their jobs. Since no tour buses or short air flights to bookings existed yet, car trips were the trio's only option. While Luther drove, Johnny filled scraps of paper with songs, outlining melodies with guitar chords, and munching on chocolate bars.

Vivian, pregnant again, stayed home with Rosanne, feeling isolated and alone. Some weeks she hardly heard more than "Hello, I love you, good-bye." Johnny would one day admit that his absences and the preoccupation with music—which his daughter Rosanne would say "originate[d] in his very cells"—hurt his marriage. "The more the world pulled me away," he explained, "the harder [Vivian] pulled in the other direction, trying to hold me in a family bond."

Driving back from Louisiana Hayride one Sunday, Johnny could almost hear the wild applause from Saturday night's audience. He had sung at a fever pitch, giving his all to every song. The *San Francisco Chronicle* printed a headline reading: "It Looks as If Elvis Has a Rival—From Arkansas." That Sunday, however, as Marshall let cars go ahead of him to turn off the road into church parking lots, Johnny felt suddenly lonesome for his Baptist upbringing. "I ought to be in church!" he announced. Luther suggested stopping, but Johnny shrugged, waving them onward. Too many miles lay ahead, and they had another show that night.

Johnny and Vivian kept arguing about the separations. He wanted to be a good husband and father. His wife was sweet to him; she had even been making his favorite "farmer food"—pork chops and runner beans—instead of her mother's Italian dishes. He imagined writing a song about faithfulness, and on tour in Texas the words poured out. Carl Perkins suggested the title "I Walk the Line," and in November the single (with "Get Rhythm" on the B-side) was released by Sam Phillips. Amazingly, the song achieved what everyone in the 1950s music business said was almost impossible—it became a crossover hit from country (#1 on the charts) to pop (#17 on the charts). Fans ate up "I Walk the Line," bringing Johnny his first gold record and first BMI (Broadcast Music Incorporated) award. The song, an anthem to fidelity, became his all-time best seller:

> I keep a close watch on this heart of mine.
> I keep my eyes wide open all the time.
> I keep the ends out for the tie that binds.
> Because you're mine, I walk the line.
>
> I find it very, very easy to be true.
> I find myself alone when each day is through.
> Yes, I'll admit that I'm a fool for you.
> Because you're mine, I walk the line.

As sure as night is dark and day is light,
I keep you on my mind both day and night.
And happiness I've known proves that it's right.
Because you're mine, I walk the line.

Johnny hummed quietly before each song verse, an innovative twist for a ballad. Within the timbre of his voice was a clear resolve to be honest, to speak his mind. The trio was in North Carolina when they heard that "I Walk the Line" had sold more than two million copies in the U.S. Hollering with glee, they decided to celebrate by eating snow cream. At the next food store, they bought a pan, a spoon, milk, sugar, eggs, and vanilla. Parking on Soco Mountain, they used newly fallen snow to mix up a batch of celebration.

Johnny's second royalty check was for almost six thousand dollars, money that would have been a fortune to his father and other Depression farmers in the mid-1930s. Now he could pay the landlady for the babysitting she had done for free, and he would have money left over after expenses for one-night gigs. He and Vivian moved from the apartment to a rented house, and then bought a house on Sandy Cove.

Kathy, their second daughter, was born on April 16, 1956. Two other daughters followed: Cindy, on July 29, 1958, and Tara, on August 24, 1961.

Slowly, Johnny was becoming comfortable chatting and joking between songs with people at his shows. He would always have a tinge of shyness with strangers and be more at ease singing than talking, but as Christopher Wren, one of his early biographers, wrote: "He learned how to seize and hold an audience that lacked the near-fanatical loyalty he was to elicit in years to come. On cramped stages, with archaic sound systems, under dim lighting, Johnny Cash became a pro."

Some of Johnny's stage jokes weren't even verbal. In Etowa, Arkansas, he pulled a comb from his jacket and ran it through his hair. Immediately, Marshall jumped past the stand-up bass, yanked away the comb, and threw it on the floor. Somehow he came up with a blank-filled pistol and shot the comb. "Lice!" Marshall screamed, and the audience burst out laughing.

When the Plymouth needed to be put out to pasture for another car, Johnny was touring with singer Ferlin Husky. He couldn't afford a pink Cadillac, or a new car off the showroom floor, so he bought Ferlin's slightly used, maroon Lincoln. Feeling "spiffy," he drove to Nashville's Ryman Auditorium to see Jim Denny, manager of the Grand Ole Opry. Big country stars like Minnie Pearl, Hank Williams, Roy Acuff, and the Carter Family were Opry regulars. Nashville was strictly traditional in its country style, and hybrid music—especially rock 'n' roll—wasn't welcome. Elvis Presley, Carl Perkins, Jerry Lee Lewis, Roy Orbison, and Johnny Cash weren't invited to perform. "It was a wonder," Johnny would say, "[that Nashville] even let us in the city limits."

Two hours passed before Jim Denny finally opened his office door for Johnny. "What makes you think you belong on the Grand Ole Opry?" Denny asked.

Johnny smiled. "Well," he said, "I love country music—always sung it—and besides that, I have a number-one country record."

He did, indeed, and Jim Denny worked out a booking for him. Onstage at the Opry on July 7, 1956, Johnny was aware that some people resented him and saw him as a music outlaw. "I Walk the Line" was too pop, they said. And some musicians were probably jealous of him. Nevertheless, the audience went crazy for Johnny Cash. His deep baritone vibrated in the balcony like a plugged-in electric wire. At the microphone, his guitar against his hip, he could have pinched himself. He couldn't believe he was a guest star at the famous Opry! A review in the next day's *Nashville Banner* said of "I Walk the Line": "The boy had struck home, where the heart is, with his song. . . ."

Johnny appeared often at the Opry, which meant he had to give up his Saturday Louisiana Hayride appearances. Traveling into Nashville meant another whirlwind schedule. The trio sometimes drove all night, arriving in Tennessee just before showtime. But if they were exhausted, they were able to hide it. "Hello, I'm Johnny Cash," Johnny would say as he walked onstage, his voice like rolling thunder. Those four words, repeated in years ahead at performances across the world, became his show-opener trademark.

The fatigue that hounded the trio on the road was nothing new to traveling musicians. Some lived out of their cars. Others, stressed over facing often rowdy, rude, or boozed-up crowds, ended up dead from car accidents, drugs, or alcohol. Both Hank Williams and

Johnny Horton, two of Johnny's music heroes, died on the road.

After a 1957 concert in Miami, Johnny and his sidekicks, along with three performers from Bob Neal's troupe, Faron Young, Ferlin Husky, and Gordon Terry, took a 350-mile trek to a booking in Jacksonville, Florida. After an hour of driving Faron's car, Gordon stopped at the side of the road. Luther, driving Johnny's used Lincoln, pulled in behind him. Sticking his head inside the Lincoln, Gordon asked Luther if he was feeling tired.

Gordon held out a hand, palm-up. "Take one of these," he told Luther. "It'll keep you awake." Squinting, Luther peered down at the tiny white pills scored with crosses.

"What are they?" Johnny asked.

"Bennies," was the reply.

"Will they hurt you?" Johnny said.

Gordon shook his head. Doctors, he said, called them amphetamines, and prescribed them for worn-out truckers and overweight people. They pepped you up, burned calories, and came in different varieties and colors. With one bennie—the L.A. Turnaround—you could drive without sleep from New York to L.A. and back again! "Here," Gordon said to Johnny, "have one. They'll make you want to go to Jacksonville and enjoy yourself after you get there."

Johnny paused, then dropped one of the little pills into his mouth. A half hour later, he was raring to go. He couldn't sleep that night, but he wasn't tired. The butterflies in his stomach that usually came before he went onstage hadn't appeared. Bennies seemed to be a good thing. Like the truckers, he would have more road energy. He could sing and play guitar until the cows came home.

Before leaving Florida, Johnny bought a whole bottle of bennies from Gordon Terry, paying less than ten dollars for one hundred pills. He was totally unaware that time would prove doctors wrong about amphetamine safety, that bennies would lead him into the hellfire he had heard about as a boy at the Baptist church in Dyess. Ultimately, for Johnny, bennies were not just pills. Inside them, hiding "at no extra cost," was a hideous "demon called Deception."

After his first show at the Grand Ole Opry in 1956, Johnny began performing there regularly.

SIX

WITH SUCCESSES PILING UP, Johnny Cash tore out of his beloved South. He was booked all over California for one-nighters by a promoter who had bought a 50 percent share of his contract from manager Bob Neal. Johnny had become hot property for any music manager. In New York City, he appeared on TV's *Jackie Gleason Show*, *The Ed Sullivan Show*, Dick Clark's *American Bandstand*, and Red Foley's *Jubilee*. He did a three-week tour in Canada, driving with the Tennessee Two over four hundred miles a day.

At first the bennies changed what was hectic for Johnny into fun and excitement. Crashes, or "downs," followed the highs, but they seemed worth it. Johnny's performances, which had been riveting from the start, gained spectacular momentum. He was more outgoing on bennies. He sang with unflagging gusto. Sometimes he pointed his guitar, as if it were a rifle, straight at the audience. Or he made fun of Luther's stiff pose over his electric guitar, joking, "Luther? Don't worry about him, he's been dead for two years!"

Vivian didn't know yet about the bennies, so she couldn't understand why Johnny was awake until dawn, pacing up and down. She had been busy answering batches of fan mail from the U.S. and Canada, and corresponding with one woman about an official fan club. Writing features for the club's newsletter, Vivian raved in print about her husband and daughters, hiding the increasing strain in the marriage. Johnny, traveling eight months out of twelve, was often irritable. When Vivian did discover pills in his dresser drawers, shirt pockets, and the glove compartment of the car, she was horrified. "She saw them as deadly right from the start," Johnny would say.

Highs from the bennies helped Johnny persuade Sam Phillips, who preferred single releases over costly albums, to produce the popular Sun album *Johnny Cash and His Hot and Blue Guitar*. Next came two new, impressively poetic Cash singles that hit the country and pop charts: "Big River" and "Give My Love to Rose," which was written by Johnny in a club near California's San Quentin Prison about a dying ex-con's last wishes:

I found him by the railroad track this morning.
I could see that he was nearly dead.
I knelt down beside him and I listened
Just to hear the words the dying fellow said.

He said they let me out of prison down in Frisco.
For ten long years I've paid for what I've done.
I was trying to get back to Louisiana
To see my Rose and get to know my son.

Chorus:
Give my love to Rose please won't you mister.
Take her all my money, tell her to buy some
  pretty clothes.
Tell my boy his daddy's so proud of him
And don't forget to give my love to Rose.

At a party in spring 1958, Johnny met Don Law, a producer at Columbia Records. The singing contract he'd signed with Sun Records before recording "Hey, Porter" was nearing renewal time, but Don wanted Johnny at Columbia. Johnny's bond with Sam Phillips was tight—Sam, he'd say, chose "soul, fire, and heart" over technical purity—but he still couldn't interest him in gospel music. Besides, Sam had added drums and vocal arrangements to recent Cash singles, diminishing the simplicity of Johnny's sound. Come to Columbia, Don Law told him. He could do gospel. He could make albums. He could sing how he wanted.

A handshake sealed the deal. But when Sam Phillips caught wind of the situation and questioned Johnny about leaving, Johnny denied it. "I don't know why I found it easy to lie to Sam about it, but that's how it was." The two men, however, never lost their affection for each other. Twenty-six years later, when a dinner and roast were held for Sam in his Alabama hometown, Johnny drove in to speak about him.

By August, Johnny had contracted with Columbia. In a smart marketing move for the company, he was given free reign to record gospel music as long as he also provided more saleable Cash songs. An album, *The Fabulous Johnny Cash*, appeared in November, selling over 400,000 copies, making the pop charts, and becoming *Billboard*'s country and western album of the year. It contained what became two of Johnny's classic hits, "I Still Miss Someone," a ballad of romantic longing, and "Don't Take Your Guns to Town," a wrenching Western tale of death:

I Still Miss Someone

At my door, the leaves are falling;
A cold, wild wind has come.
Sweethearts walk by together,
And I still miss someone. . . .

Don't Take Your Guns to Town

He drank his first strong liquor then to calm his
shaking hand,
And tried to tell himself he had become a man.
A dusty cowpoke at his side began to laugh him down,
And he heard again his mother's words:

Chorus:
Don't take your guns to town, son.
Leave your guns at home, Bill.
Don't take your guns to town. . . .

Johnny's second Columbia album was released in 1959, and it was what he'd been waiting for—gospel. *Hymns by Johnny Cash* featured old standards like "Swing Low Sweet Chariot" as well as several original songs, one of which, "I Call Him," was written by Johnny and his father together. In another 1959 album, *Songs of Our Soil*, Johnny's "The Old Apache Squaw" touched on the suffering of Native American Indians. This was the beginning of Johnny's passionate diatribe against mistreatment of Native Americans. Music critic Stephen Miller, in writing of Johnny's early Columbia songs, described his "solemn, reflective" tone that showed "a maturity beyond his twenty-seven years."

Johnny filled concert halls with cheering fans. His earnings had tripled, but in his pockets were the bennies, prescribed by doctors listed in the Yellow Pages or slipped to him by druggists or friends. He tried all the varieties and colors. He'd go for days without his demon drugs, but then, with big shows to do and thousands of people expecting his best, he swallowed Benzedrine, Dexedrine, or Dexamyl. If he couldn't "wear the pills out" before needing sleep, he took barbiturates, or tranquilizers. "From time to time," he wrote later, "I'd worry a bit that the pills were beginning to hurt me, but I'd take another pill and I wouldn't worry anymore."

Luther and Marshall, watching Johnny, stood helplessly on the sidelines. Johnny's eyes were dilated, he had spasms in his neck and face, and he couldn't stay still. He sometimes forgot what he was saying. Coming off highs, he felt like briers or wood splinters were embedded in him. They seemed alive, "twitching and squirming" in his flesh. He wanted desperately to pluck them out, but of course he couldn't. "Then," he wrote later, "I *had* to take more pills."

A drying agent in the amphetamines, combined with cigarettes and beer, gave him laryngitis. If he couldn't talk above a whisper, he canceled shows, ashamed and angry. His friend Roger Miller, the pop singing star, once did four shows for him in Las Vegas. Another friend, country singer Merle Kilgore (who also took drugs), gave him an open invitation to crash at his apartment. But after many nights of pounding on Merle's door, Johnny was no longer welcome.

Vivian, who'd given birth now to a third daughter, Cindy, had pleaded with him to stop taking the pills, but he hadn't. He couldn't even fool Jack. His brother often came to him in dreams, a preacher just as he'd pledged to their mother. He asked Johnny to redeem himself.

His highs were sometimes followed by moody lows and, "burdened down with guilt," he'd pray for strength to heal himself. One night in California, he drove a jeep across a salt flat and up a hill, veering around desert bushes until he reached the top. He couldn't see down the other side, but he didn't care.

"I dare you," Johnny suddenly shouted in the jeep, "to turn off your lights and go down the other side." He took his own dare, but not before flipping open a beer, drinking it down, then drinking another. Dizzy, his fists clenched on the steering wheel, he let the jeep catapult down the hill. As it tumbled forward, it smashed against large boulders and bushes. "By moonlight," he would write, "I could see [that] . . . darkness lay straight ahead."

The jeep hurtled into a grove of trees and manzanita bushes. With his fingers still gripping the wheel, Johnny flung himself back against the seat until the jeep jolted to a stop. Amazingly, he was only bruised. Stunned at the risk he'd taken and somehow survived, he could hardly unbend his fingers. His knuckles were white, like bones with no skin. He swallowed two bennies and, with the jeep clanking, drove away.

That April 1959, Johnny traveled to Australia for his first overseas tour. Nineteen thousand people pushed into a concert hall to hear him, and thirty thousand more came the next day. In his black pants, shirt, and boots, he looked to many like someone you wouldn't mess with. Tickets to his shows sold out, leaving standing room only.

Were his demons listening? In just four years as a singer, Johnny Cash had, in spite of his battle with deadly drugs, sold an astounding six million records.

Most managers and promoters of big-time singers wanted their clients' home base to be New York or Hollywood. Johnny's second manager, Stew Carnall, talked up Hollywood—its nightclubs, ballrooms, concert halls, even movie roles. Johnny had logged so much time in California that he agreed in 1958 to move from Memphis to L.A. Luther and Marshall would follow him, but they stayed only a year, preferring to travel from Tennessee to appear anywhere with Johnny. By then, Johnny's success had made him "hotter than a two-dollar pistol," and he could demand the best backup guitarists in the business. But he didn't. He liked things the way they were; he, Luther, and Marshall were the good ole boys. He did, however, hire a drummer, a former air-conditioning repairman named W. S. "Fluke" Holland, who'd played drums for Carl Perkins. The Tennessee Two became the Tennessee Three.

Johnny drove the eighteen hundred miles to California with Vivian, three-year-old Rosanne, two-year-old Kathy, and baby Cindy. He rented an apartment in North Hollywood where Cindy slept in a dresser drawer. Several months later, he paid $75,000 (a lot of money at the time) for TV talk show host Johnny Carson's house in Encino, a Los Angeles suburb. He also bought a trailer park in nearby Ojai and moved his parents to California to manage it.

Johnny was living light years away from the lean Dyess days; he had earned a quarter of a million dollars in 1959. Paid after each concert, he put off going to the bank. He was a singer, he'd say, not a businessman. Once, he left $7,100 in a jar for weeks. When money lay around the house, Rosanne and Kathy sometimes put it in the washing machine.

Johnny did receive a Hollywood movie role, though in a grade-B murder thriller that was a flop. He starred as a psychotic killer in *Five Minutes to Live* (later renamed *Door-to-Door Maniac*). The leading lady was the producer's wife. He also made guest appearances on four TV Westerns: *Tales of Wells Fargo*, *Shotgun Slade*, *Wagon*

Train, and *The Rebel* (for which he sang the title song).

He was now booked for two hundred shows a year, traveling a 300,000-mile circuit, and singing to over one million people. Fans who saw his black outfits and heard his songs of desperate men and desperate deeds dubbed him "The Man in Black." Johnny liked the name. He had always felt at ease with that color.

In 1960, he obtained the go-ahead from Columbia to record what he called a "concept album" or "country opera," *Ride This Train*, using an innovative format of choosing album songs around a central theme. His five concept albums, all popular and successful, were songs and stories of America, its land, religion, trains, hard work, courage, and sorrows. In *Ride This Train*, listeners are introduced to lumberjacks, miners, prisoners, a plantation owner, and a rural doctor. The backdrop for many songs is the mesmerizing sound of a steam engine or of hammers pounding rocks and nails. Author Michael McCall recognized the historical basis of *Ride This Train*: "Cash tied it all together with narration that sounded as if it could come from an old schoolroom documentary on American life."

When he wasn't recording or performing, Johnny didn't rush home to Encino. He went fishing or jammed with friends, not wanting to face Vivian or his little girls. The pills kept dealing their old tricks of dark lows following the highs, so he needed more of them. Ten a day became twenty, then thirty, then fifty. He never did hard drugs or marijuana, but people like Johnny who had naïvely tried amphetamines could be dangerously hooked. In the 1960s, 100,000 pounds of amphetamines were either prescribed or "pushed" each year in the United States. Users gave them nicknames like "little jewels," "popcorn," and "old yellers."

Johnny's restlessness wasn't entirely new. Back in Dyess, he had been a fidgety little boy, racing along the Tyronza River. And after losing Jack, despair and anger had joined his jitters. Now addicted to the little jewels, and wanting to sing almost more than to breathe, he turned his restlessness into concocting outrageous pranks with his friends.

Practical jokes on the road were a quick fix for boredom. Marshall, who neither smoked nor drank, was hailed by Johnny, Luther, Fluke Holland, Gordon Terry, and manager Stew Carnall as "The Mad Bomber" because he crafted his own explosives. Over one week, aside from setting off firecrackers, Marshall wrapped enough twine around sticks of dynamite to make a basketball-sized wad. Then he shellacked the twine. "I'm making a bomb," he said. At the New Mexico–Texas border, the group dumped the bomb in the desert, sprinkled a long line of black gunpowder back to the road as a do-it-yourself fuse, then lit a match to it. The explosion caused a few desert dwellers to claim a meteor had hit earth. And near Tyler, Texas, another of Marshall's bombs had enough kick to make telephone wires vibrate for miles.

With Marshall as the Mad Bomber, Gordon Terry oversaw "interior decorating." In motel rooms, he might paint walls, ceilings, furniture—even mirrors—black for the Man in Black. Johnny, however, would paint the black-and-white TV screen bright red. He liked color TV, he'd say, willing to pay for the damages. Laughing hysterically, the group would wait for the look on the maid's face when she came to clean. And the manager? He usually just collected an extra fifty or one hundred dollars. After all, Johnny Cash had signed the register. You know, that guy in black with the really deep voice and the songs that ate your heart out.

Johnny got handy at sawing legs off motel tables, then gluing them back just enough so they'd collapse the next day when dusted. He used a fire ax to chop a "doorway" in a wall between adjoining rooms. He checked into hotels and handed bellhops a small suitcase filled with lead weights weighing over one hundred pounds. Before checking out of one hotel, he filled the bathtub with hot water and Jell-O.

In Iowa, Johnny and his good ole boys sneaked two hundred feet of rope into a hotel room. Near dawn, they crawled down the seventh-floor corridor and tied all the doorknobs together. Before racing to their rooms, they knocked on the doors to awaken guests. Frantic phone calls to the front desk finally brought a clerk upstairs with a pair of scissors.

Gordon Terry, who had recorded a novelty song, "Johnson's Old Grey Mule," could bray with ear-shattering volume. In the courtyard of a Minneapolis hotel, he let out a huge bray while Marshall fired a cap-and-ball gun. Guests thought a donkey had been shot. And at the fancy Waldorf-Astoria in New York City, Johnny and Stew Carnall bought hay and buckets of manure from a Central Park riding stable. After dragging them from a service elevator into their room, they spread the mixture over the entire floor. One troupe member noted that although the furnishings were beautiful, the room looked like a horse "had been living there for a week."

By the 1970s, rock bands like The Who and Led Zeppelin were also trashing some of their surroundings. Drugs, liquor, rage, boredom, and too much success too soon often led to misconduct. Many hotels stopped renting rooms to show-business rebels. For Johnny, his transgressions continued until he confronted what he labeled his "miserable streak."

Neither his addiction nor destructive behavior had been reported in newspapers or on television. According to biographer Christopher Wren, they stayed "locked within the country music trade." But in 1961, at three thirty A.M. on a Nashville street, his secrets started to leak out. Several policemen arrested him for trying to kick down the door of a nightclub he claimed wouldn't let him in. The club was actually closed, and Johnny, high on pills, spent four hours in jail. A headline in the next day's *Nashville Banner* read: "Johnny Cash Arrested Here on Drunk Charge."

While burgeoning crowds clapped and shouted for Johnny all over the world, and while his newest record albums and singles flashed like meteors up the pop and country charts, he kept straying into a wilderness that would oppress him for ten years and lock him behind bars seven times.

LIFE

JOHNNY CASH
The Rough-cut King
of Country Music

Johnny Cash sings
of trains, prisons
and hard times

NOVEMBER 21 · 1969 · 40¢

The November 21, 1969, issue of LIFE magazine featured Johnny.

SEVEN

IN STARKVILLE, MISSISSIPPI, Johnny was hauled into jail in 1965 for picking flowers at two A.M. on private property. He beat against the jail bars all night, and his cell was later called the Johnny Cash Suite. Other pill-related arrests happened in Nevada, Texas, California, and Georgia. Yet Johnny, wanting to give something back to the lost souls in society, made music history by also playing benefit performances in prisons: Texas State Prison in Huntsville, Cummins in Arkansas, Hutchinson in Kansas, Folsom and San Quentin in California.

At the Texas prison, Johnny, Luther, and Marshall performed in a giant rainstorm. Luther's amplifier shorted out, and Marshall's bass was so wet that it fell apart. But Johnny, soaked and shivering, kept on playing and singing. The convicts loved him for it.

And he, locked in his own prison of pills, didn't feel like an outsider. When he performed at Cummins, he had been fighting for prison reform and for justice for American Indians, both in and out of jail. He prompted Governor Winthrop Rockefeller of Arkansas to contribute ten thousand dollars to help build a chapel for the convicts, and he donated five thousand dollars of his own.

Though the strain in his marriage had continued, Johnny bought fifteen hillside acres in Casitas Springs, northwest of Ventura, California, to build a new family home. The rural area seemed good for Rosanne, who'd suffered from allergies in Encino. A contractor, Curly Lewis, built the Cashes a five-bedroom ranch house, which was completed just after Tara, their fourth daughter, was born. The girls were isolated on the hill, but Johnny liked it because he felt free to go shooting there. He erected a lighted, ten-foot-high cross on the house that he took down at Easter and loaned to a local church. At Christmas, he attached a huge amplifier to the roof, blasting carols down the hillside into the community, pleasing some residents but annoying others—and bringing out sheriff's deputies.

Shrugging, Johnny yanked a plug out of the amplifier midway through "Joy to the World."

He got himself a camper in Casitas Springs, painting the side windows black, and naming it Jesse after the outlaw Jesse James. Aching and high on pills, with a flashlight and gun at his side, he would drive into the desert or Death Valley, sleeping in Jesse after he stopped prowling at night through cactus and brush. He sometimes took Curly Lewis along, but after five or six trips Curly was too disturbed by Johnny's manic episodes to go with him again.

On one outing in the Mojave Desert, Ray Cash joined his son and Curly in the camper. Johnny had swallowed handfuls of pills. Spying a sign off the main highway reading NO TRESPASSING—U.S. NAVAL PROVING GROUNDS—U.S.N. ORDINANCE, he drove through the locked gate. Several miles of dirt road led him onto land full of deep craters, torn-up military trucks, and scattered shrapnel.

"We're on a bombing and strafing range!" Curly said.

"[We're] going to get into trouble in here," Ray warned.

The navy officer with a rifle who soon ordered them off government property said he'd expected to see the camper blown to bits by mines. Johnny's father was too worried over the perils of Johnny's drugs to tell Carrie Cash about the trip.

Jesse the camper met the same fate as all of Johnny's vehicles during his ten-year pill dependence—it was destroyed beyond what even Luther and Marshall could repair. Once, on a frenzied lurch down a mountain, Johnny broke his jaw when Jesse flipped over, making singing dates very difficult. The Cash wreckage list included Johnny's cars, two jeeps, Jesse, two boats that sank in two separate lake accidents, and a truck from which he jumped before it plunged over a six-hundred-foot California cliff.

Hoping to redeem himself, as Jack still urged in his dreams, Johnny joined the Avenue Community Church. He had occasionally wandered into churches over recent years, kneeling in pews with his pockets temporarily empty of pills. But then he meandered away, and his visits were only sporadic. The pastor at Avenue Community Church, Floyd Gressett, worked in prisons and knew the ravages of drugs. He took Johnny fishing and, sympathizing with his struggles, gave him a key to his California ranch house in Cuyuma Valley. With humor, Gressett nicknamed Johnny "Slick," and in return, Johnny called him "Chief."

An unstated pact existed between the two men. Johnny never admitted he was on pills, and Gressett never accused him of it. "He was wise enough to know," Johnny would write, "that a man taking drugs isn't going to listen to you. And if he's acting like he's listening, he's very likely not listening. And I wasn't listening—not yet."

So Johnny came to church, singing and playing guitar for the congregation, and Gressett picked up the pieces when Johnny was in Casitas Springs but not at services. Hunting him down, Gressett might find him in the camper, senseless from days without food. He would drive him to Cuyuma Valley, feed him, and put him to bed. He would talk quietly about Vivian and the children, a pastor's reminder of family responsibility.

One day, Johnny would apologize to Vivian for the pain he had caused her. "I had gone too far," he said, "stayed away too much." As for his daughters, he would always regret what he missed of their childhood. Too often he forgot birthdays, holidays, or school events;

he was too high (he was hearing voices now) or too low to call from the road to say good night. He loved his daughters but had less and less of himself to give. "For all practical purposes," he'd explain, "my girls lost a daddy, and their daddy was coming closer and closer to losing his mortal and spiritual life."

Drugs, however, didn't obliterate the genius of his music. Slips of paper were still crowded with songs he wrote, revised, and wrote again. His third manager, a Canadian producer named Saul Holiff, kept booking him into big European clubs and concert halls. A new concept album, *Ballads of the True West*, gave listeners a deeper appreciation of America and its heritage. Even if some of the songs Johnny composed while drugs ravaged his brain weren't up to snuff, many of them showed stunning clarity, depth, originality, and passion.

While his demon pills had power beyond measure, part of Johnny wanted to defy them. Clutching at straws, he planted a cupful of cotton seeds on his land in Casitas Springs. They brought him sharp memories of Dyess—its grueling work, its righteous piety, and the same sense of moral responsibility urged by Floyd

Gressett. He was living in California and bringing his songs to the most sophisticated cities in the world, but at heart he was really a country boy from the southern side of the Mason-Dixon Line.

Band music, rollicking and grand, was popular in the 1960s, and Johnny's addiction didn't cloud his ability to see country and pop trends. He arranged for a small group of country artists to travel and perform with him and the Tennessee Three, the entire troupe called the Johnny Cash Show. The first additions were the popular gospel and country singers, the Statler Brothers: Harold Reid, Phil Balsley, Don Reid, and Lew DeWitt. They had picked their name from a box of Statler tissues in a New York hotel room. "We might have been called the Kleenex Brothers," Harold joked. Then came June Carter of the legendary Carter Family, her mother Maybelle, and her two sisters, Anita and Helen. Along with singing, the four women, who toured with Elvis in the mid-1950s, played autoharp, guitar, banjo, and mandolin.

The original Carter Family—A. P. Carter, his wife Sara, and Sara's cousin Maybelle—pioneered country harmony singing within the old mountain tradition of purely instrumental music. On his travels, A. P. Carter collected hundreds of country, folk, and gospel songs, many of which became the basis of modern American country music: "Will the Circle Be Unbroken," "Wildwood Flower," "Keep on the Sunny Side." The Carters grew up in Clinch Valley, Virginia, an Appalachian area near the Tennessee border. A. P., Sara, and Maybelle—"the first family of country music," according to music historians and critics—began recording in 1927 and toured until 1943.

Maybelle, known as Mother Maybelle in the music industry, continued the Carter Family in the 1940s with her three daughters, who were so young they had to stand on boxes to reach the microphone. She was revered for inventing a technique, the "Carter lick," on her acoustic six-string guitar that involved strumming chords on higher strings while simultaneously picking melodies on lower ones. Her creation, Johnny explained to crowds when Maybelle played on his shows, was "the most influential guitar style in country and folk music." In 1966, the Grand Ole Opry honored Maybelle Carter as the Mother of Country Music, and in 1970 she was inducted into the Country Music Hall of Fame.

Johnny first saw June Carter onstage when his Dyess senior class attended the Grand Ole Opry. Twenty-one-year-old June, dark-haired, spunky, and beautiful, did country-style comedy between songs. "Sit down," she'd say to audiences, "squat down, lie down, but honey, make yourself at home!" Six years later, Johnny was performing alongside June at the Opry. He was married to Vivian, and June, divorced from country singer Carl Smith, was married to garage owner Rip Nix.

Impulsively, Johnny greeted the gorgeous young Opry star with the words, "You and I are going to get married someday." June Carter was no shrinking violet. At age ten, though her church condemned dancing, she danced alone in the woods, waving a swatch of chiffon. At fourteen, she drove a two-and-a-half-ton lumber truck. Laughing at Johnny Cash's audacity, June replied, "Well, good. I can't wait." In the second of his two autobiographies, Johnny wrote about this exchange: "And there went the seed, in the ground."

The first performance of the Johnny Cash Show was at the Big D Jamboree in Dallas. Outside the U.S. and Canada, Johnny's new troupe flew together to bookings; otherwise, they traveled in a Johnny Cash bus named Unit One. Johnny's newest single, "Seasons of My Heart," had made the pop chart Top Ten, and his concept album *Blood, Sweat and Tears* honored the working man and folk hero John Henry and his steel-drivin' hammer.

Some concerts, however, were being canceled again—enough in the early 1960s to worry his family, friends, the troupe, and Saul Holiff. Irate concert-hall and arena impresarios lost many thousands of dollars. People noticed that Johnny was twenty pounds thinner. He had always sung from one side of his mouth, but now his face visibly contorted when he sang. Fans, however, didn't pause long over it. His voice swept away everything else.

Soon after joining the troupe, June Carter realized Johnny was on pills. She had been close to country-music star Hank Williams before he died from an addiction. She had prayed daily for Hank, and she prayed now for Johnny. When he crashed off highs, she countered his moodiness with her optimism and sidestepped the pranks that made him seem like a lost child. When he and Marshall set off cherry bombs in a parking lot, she stayed mum. Her true introduction to the mayhem came when Johnny, Marshall, and Luther gave her "an official welcome." They crashed into her hotel room, declaring how happy they were with her, then dumped a barrel of confetti knee-deep on the floor.

"Lord, what are you doing?" she asked, climbing onto her bed.

"Don't worry, June," reassured Johnny. "We'll clean it up. We want to show you how good we are at cleanin' things up."

Marshall and Fluke Holland rolled in a lawn mower borrowed from a hotel employee and proceeded to suck up the confetti until the mower ran out of gas. June shooed the men away and spent the rest of the day sweeping. The confetti, she said that night in her prayers, must have been what she called her "initiation ceremony."

In 1962, Johnny's booking at New York's Carnegie Hall was a historic chance to bring rural American songs to patrons of classical music. The media flooded him with TV, magazine, and newspaper interviews. Before the concert, however, he went on a reckless, pill-drenched moose hunt with Gordon Terry and singer/songwriter Merle Travis. Onstage at Carnegie Hall, Johnny barely had a voice. He struggled through a medley of Jimmie Rodgers songs, which were not what the audience wanted to hear. Responding to shouted requests for "I Walk the Line," "Don't Take Your Guns to Town," and "Folsom Prison Blues," he hoarsely whispered his way through them. "It was awful," he'd say, "from start to finish." Don Law, his Columbia Records producer, never turned on the recording equipment set up for a planned live album of the performance. Newspaper reviews were biting.

That winter, Johnny volunteered to sing for U.S. soldiers who had fought in the Korean War and remained there to uphold the 1953 armistice. During the tour, he and his troupe performed before twenty-six thousand GIs, about half of all the soldiers stationed in Korea. He felt proud of the men who had risked their lives. He pushed himself to crowd in more shows, and the prearranged twenty stretched to thirty. "Johnny, Johnny, Johnny!" the men yelled to him. "We're walkin' the line!" But back in California after the exhausting tour, he had such severe laryngitis, he was hospitalized. Thin and pale, he lost his voice completely for several weeks.

June Carter and Marshall were Johnny's unofficial rescue squad. They spied on him and shored him up when he needed it. June finally confronted him after Korea about the pills. He was tough enough, she told him, to survive without them. On tours, she ironed his shirts and sewed loose buttons, and Johnny was comforted by her presence. But not always. When he hid pills in a toothbrush case, but they were gone when he opened it; when he slid a bag of pills inside a rip in his car's upholstery, but it disappeared, he realized someone was stealing from him. That someone, he knew, was June Carter, feisty, brave, and generous—and willing to oppose him when he couldn't find his bennies.

Johnny and June's relationship seesawed. Sometimes he actually thanked her for sneaking into his hotel room, rummaging through his belongings, and flushing any pills she found down the toilet. She had helped him, he said. But other times, sweating and hurting, he violently tore everything from drawers, hunting for his demons so that even if he couldn't think straight, he could still sing. Then he wasn't so thankful. He demanded his "property," he accused June of meddling. But although he was mad, he still thought of her as an avenging angel. And he could imagine that, somewhere, his brother Jack and Floyd Gressett were smiling.

In one of his most livid outbursts, his suitcase empty of pills and his room cleaned out, Johnny turned to June and yelled, "If you weren't a woman, I'd break your neck."

She stared at him, unflinching. She had two young daughters in Nashville—Carlene and Rosey—who knew that steely look. June and the Carter Family, who were deeply spiritual, had traveled with Johnny for a year now and had seen his best and his worst. They had marked the deep well of kindness in him, the humor, the shyness around strangers, the voice that shook the earth with its songs. His Baptist faith had grappled with an unbearable childhood loss. Now, addicted to a poison and often out of touch with his God, he was fighting for his life.

June smiled and raised an eyebrow. "You'd miss me," she said. He didn't need more than a second to know she was right.

EIGHT

JOHNNY WAS NEVER permanently sucked into the mud of his addiction. Even if Luther, Marshall, or Fluke had to push him onstage after he'd dulled a nerve-jangling high with too many beers, there he was: the Man in Black. Author Charles Paul Conn described him as "barely able to stand at the microphone, [and] somehow still generating more musical excitement than anyone in the audience could remember ever feeling before."

By the mid-1960s, Columbia had released Johnny's singles "Understand Your Man," "Mean as Hell," "Happy to Be with You," and "Ring of Fire," plus the albums *The Christmas Spirit*, *Keep on the Sunny Side*, *Bitter Tears: Ballads of the American Indian*, *Ballads of the True West*, *Orange Blossom Special*, and *Ring of Fire—The Best of Johnny Cash*. The single of "Ring of Fire," written in 1962 by June Carter and Merle Kilgore, was originally recorded by June's sister Anita. Johnny also recorded the song, but waited six months so he didn't compete with Anita's folk version ("Love's Burning Ring of Fire").

Before writing "Ring of Fire," June Carter realized she was falling in love with Johnny. She felt anguish over it, even though her own marriage was already failing. Johnny, she kept reminding herself, had a family, and when he was high on pills, he was a hellion. He could be as stubborn as the two-and-a-half-ton truck she'd driven at age fourteen. He was like no one she'd ever met. And June's lyrics in "Ring of Fire" weren't lost on Johnny Cash.

Months before he recorded the song, Johnny dreamed one night of having trumpets accompany it. Historically, horns weren't used in country music, and the record company was against the idea, but he insisted. His "Ring of Fire," with its trademark mariachi horns, reached #1 on the country charts, #17 on the pop charts, and won a Columbia Gold Guitar Award. Like "I Walk the Line" and "Folsom Prison Blues," the song became a Johnny Cash classic:

Love is a burning thing
And it makes a fiery ring
Bound by wild desire
I fell into a ring of fire.

Chorus:
I fell into a burning ring of fire
I went down, down, down
And the flames went higher.
And it burns, burns, burns
The ring of fire
The ring of fire.

The taste of love is sweet
When hearts like ours meet.
I fell for you like a child.
Oh, but the fire went wild.

Johnny returned June's feelings but hadn't told her yet. His own marriage was at the breaking point and, blaming himself, he clung harder to his music.

In 1963, in New York's Gaslight Café, he met Native American singer/songwriter Peter La Farge.

Having already written "The Old Apache Squaw" and researched many tragedies suffered by Cherokee and Apache tribes, Johnny was struck anew by the prejudice often shown toward non-whites. In his fourth concept album, *Bitter Tears*, he included some of La Farge's Indian protest songs. His version of "The Ballad of Ira Hayes," written by La Farge, was a stunning #3 hit.

Ira Hayes, a poverty-stricken Pima Indian, enlisted in World War II's Marine Corps. After fierce fighting at Iwo Jima, he, four other marines, and one sailor raised the U.S. flag over the island. A famous image of the event, captured by a news photographer, was issued on U.S. postal stamps. Promoted to corporal before his discharge, Ira had a hero's welcome in America, but prejudice against his Indian heritage stopped him from finding work. Homeless and alcoholic, he died at age thirty-two in a ditch filled with two inches of water.

> *Down the ditches for a thousand years*
> *The water grew Ira's people's crops*
> *Till the white man stole the water rights*
> *And the sparklin' water stopped.*

Now Ira's folks were hungry
And their land grew crops of weeds.
When war came, Ira volunteered
And forgot the white man's greed.

Chorus:
Call him drunken Ira Hayes.
He won't answer anymore.
Not the whiskey drinkin' Indian,
Nor the Marine that went to war.

"The Ballad of Ira Hayes" caused a landmark battle within the music world. In Johnny's rendition of the song, which opens with a mournful flute playing "Taps," his fury over the treatment of Ira Hayes is obvious. "I meant every word, too," he'd say later. "I was long past the point of pulling my punches." Some DJs wouldn't play the song, saying it was too dark and criticized "white people." Disgusted, Johnny paid for a brash and unprecedented ad in the August 22, 1964, issue of *Billboard*. In it, he asked the DJs "Where are your guts?" and accused them of "wallow[ing] in their meaninglessness." An editor of one country-music magazine reacted by demanding Johnny's resignation from the Country Music Association. Fans, however, loved "The Ballad of Ira Hayes" and implored radio stations to play it.

One year later, Johnny wrote a civil-rights song called "All of God's Children Ain't Free." And when his folk singer friend Bob Dylan was lambasted in *Broadside* magazine for using an electric guitar instead of the traditional acoustic, Johnny defended him, too, writing the editors to "Shut up! . . . And let him sing!"

By 1965, Johnny had lost another twenty pounds. His bond with June had deepened, but he still resisted her efforts to get him off pills, especially when he was in the "dark, bad places" inside himself. June shooed away anyone who came backstage with a black bag and furtive look who might be supplying amphetamines. Johnny rarely went home now to Casitas Springs. Off tour, he hung out in Nashville hotels or with June's parents in nearby Madison. Maybelle Carter and her husband Ezra adored him but feared he was headed for an early grave. They gave Johnny keys to their house, telling him that even if they were traveling, he could stay.

On nights when his knees shook and his arms jerked, Johnny would lurch into Madison. He had lost the Carters' keys, of course, so if no one answered the door, he kicked it in or broke a window. The next morning, he wrote apologetic notes and left money for repairs. Sometimes he fixed the front door himself. Maybelle and Ezra stuck by him.

"I was hard on things," Johnny would write of those days. "I kicked them, I punched them, I smashed them . . ." He never physically hurt anyone, but behind his addiction, gnawing at him always, was the heavy load of sadness and outrage he carried over Jack.

One Saturday night in 1965, performing at the Grand Ole Opry, Johnny tried to remove the microphone from its stand, but it stuck. Angry, frustrated, and high, he dragged it along the footlights, shattering more than sixty bulbs. Glass flew into the audience, and the orchestra stopped playing. The manager banned him from performing again at the Opry. Strung out and stunned, he left the building, drove off in June's Cadillac, and crashed into a utility pole. The pole fell, and its electrical wires sizzled in puddles. Johnny had broken his nose and jaw, and his upper teeth slashed into his lip.

The lowest point that year came after he heard about black-market pills in Juarez, Mexico. He flew to El Paso and hired a cabbie to drive him over the border, then waited while the driver ran into a filthy bar for the drugs. Back in his hotel room, Johnny dumped 668 tablets of Dexedrine and 475 of Equanil, a tranquilizer, into two socks. He hid one under his suitcase lining and the other in his guitar. At the El Paso airport, he boarded a plane for a nine P.M. flight, but two undercover policemen who had seen him cross the border escorted him off the plane into an empty room in the terminal.

Marshall Grant, Johnny, Carl Perkins, June Carter, Anita Carter, and Helen Carter performing for a television show filmed at the Ryman Auditorium, August 30, 1968.

His stash of hidden pills was discovered, but the policemen were hunting for heroin, a known staple of Juarez drug merchants. Johnny thought he might be off the hook, and he reminded the policemen that amphetamines and tranquilizers were legal.

"But you got them illegally," the policemen said. "We'll have to book you."

He spent the remainder of the night in an El Paso jail cell with a small army of cockroaches. News of the arrest spread quickly in the media, and Sam Phillips, Don Law, and a songwriter friend, Neal Merritt, called to offer money for bail. Johnny, however, was too embarrassed to accept their help. Knowing how low he had sunk, he tried to pray. He'd let the demons drag him *down, down, down,* just like June's words in "Ring of Fire." But this time the fire was dishonor, not love.

The next morning, Marshall Grant posted bond for his friend, and Johnny was led, in handcuffs, to the courthouse for release. Flashbulbs went off in his face, and soon a photo of a handcuffed, somber Johnny Cash appeared in newspapers across the world.

He had become one of the greatest entertainers of all time, but on that October 5, 1965, he could almost hear the question from the old gospel hymn his mother had sung on the family's first freezing night in Dyess: "What Would You Give in Exchange for Your Soul?"

In 1966, in spite of her religious beliefs, Vivian Cash finally filed for divorce. Johnny had nothing but good things to say about his wife. When the decree was final in 1968, Vivian had custody of the girls and soon remarried. Also in 1966, June Carter divorced her second husband.

Many fans who read about Johnny's arrest sent notes of prayer and support to *The Legend*, the official publication of the worldwide Johnny Cash Society. They surged into his concerts, waiting to hear "Hello, I'm Johnny Cash," transfixed by his black frock coat and studded boots. He and June often sang together, and the magic between them brought yells for encores. Columbia released an album of their duets, *Carryin' On with Johnny Cash & June Carter*, which hit #5 on the country charts. Their single, "Jackson," was a crossover country/pop hit. June was his "prayer warrior," Johnny would say, someone who took people under her wing, and encouraged them with her prayers. She would fight for Johnny, she promised him, "with all her might, however she could."

When he missed bookings (a startling five in a row in the winter of 1967), Johnny's troupe filled in for him, even though they rarely got paid by agents. Once, when he didn't show up for a night concert, June and Marshall found him, hollow-eyed and hungover, fishing alone on a lake in a motorboat owned by Ezra Carter.

Looking at himself in a mirror, Johnny saw a "walking vision of death" looking back, but he yelled at it to go away. Many of his songs, wrestling with what writer Ben Ratliff called a "marrow of sadness," still gave hope of salvation. In 1967, wanting to create something steadfast in the face of pain, he sang at Wounded Knee, the South Dakota site of the last, bone-chilling massacre in 1890 of Lakota Indians. His concert helped poverty-stricken Sioux raise money for a school.

The planning stages of his concept album *From Sea to Shining Sea*, which was a musical travelogue of American life, took Johnny by foot or in his jeep along backwoods trails in Tennessee, the gullies thick with mesquite bushes, or to libraries where he read books on American history and old firearms and coins.

Nights on the trails brought him sharp memories of his daughters. How often, when he had paced the halls in the house in Casitas Springs, coming down off pills, he'd heard Vivian whispering to a crying child, "Daddy is sick. . . . Daddy is tired."

He roomed in Nashville with country singer Waylon Jennings, but Waylon advised him to buy his own home so that his girls, now twelve, eleven, nine, and six, could visit him. And in spring 1967, he found an unfinished house built into a hill above Old Hickory Lake in Hendersonville, twenty miles north of Nashville. Two round, thirty-five-foot rooms, one on top of the other, sat at each end of the stone house, and the rafters were pioneer barn timbers. Johnny made an immediate offer, but Braxton Dixon, the contractor, had no intention of selling. That is, until he and Johnny communed over a beer on the grass. They agreed on a price—$150,000—and after Johnny said he wasn't much for signing contracts, they shook hands.

If he wasn't touring, Johnny holed up at the house, stomping out cigarette butts on the floor. Though the limestone walls and the wood soothed him, pills warped his behavior. If the phone rang, he yanked it from the wall and hurled it in the lake. After he sobered up, he bought another phone. Losing keys again, he used an ax one night to chop through the front door. Now the note of apology was left for Braxton Dixon, who had become his friend and loved the house. Braxton, like June when she visited, cased the rooms for pills, flushing sockfuls down toilets.

Two incidents near the end of 1967 finally brought Johnny to the end of his ten-year nightmare. Musicians gossiped on Music Row, saying that drugs were destroying Johnny Cash, that he'd soon be dead. When he couldn't stand himself any longer, he drove to Nickajack Cave near Chattanooga, Tennessee, where Andrew Jackson and his army had slaughtered Nickajack Indians. Taking a flashlight, he dove into the network of caves that ran for miles under the mountains. He had to stop dueling with his demons, he told himself. He planned to crawl until his batteries gave out, then lie down and wait to die. Somewhere in the slime of the cave depths, however, he sensed a forgiving presence. "I thought I'd left [God]," he'd say later, "but He hadn't left me."

The pledge to God that Johnny had made in church at age twelve with Jack beside him was renewed. He didn't want to die. He began crawling in another direction, feeling the ground with his hands to avoid plunging down caverns. After more than an hour, he saw daylight, and a breeze touched his shoulder. As he left Nickajack Cave, he knew that he was meant to die only in God's time, not his own. At that moment, he felt cleansed.

A month later, just when it seemed he might be beating his drugs, Johnny was arrested on a high in Lafayette, Georgia. Two deputies locked him in jail overnight, and Sheriff Ralph Jones, a huge fan who had collected every Johnny Cash record, confronted him the next morning. The sheriff threw Johnny's money and pills on a desk. Arresting his hero hurt, so Sheriff Jones told Johnny to get out of town, take his "dope" with him, and do whatever he wanted—kill himself or quit drugs.

To Johnny, Sheriff Jones was a spokesman for the forgiving presence he had sensed in Nickajack Cave. Back in Nashville, he talked to June about his "amphetamine insanity." Mother Maybelle, he reminded her, had once sent him to meet Nat Winston, a banjo-playing psychiatrist and former commissioner of mental health for Tennessee. Could June call him? Oh, yes, came the answer.

Nat Winston agreed to come the next evening to the Hendersonville house. But Johnny—who had been off drugs for two days—found a bottle of pills hidden in the bathroom. He swallowed a handful, threw on his topcoat, and went out to drive his tractor along the cliff above Old Hickory Lake. He was steering erratically at the edge when the ground gave way, hurtling him off the tractor and into the lake. The tractor plunged into the water, barely missing him.

Coughing and flailing his arms, Johnny threw himself toward the dirt bank at cliff side, but his topcoat weighed him down. He heard a shout and saw Braxton Dixon kneeling on the bank, holding out a hand. Behind him were June and Nat Winston. He was hauled from the water and into the house. His pills were confiscated, his wet clothes removed, and he was put to bed.

Nat Winston explained to June and Braxton that Johnny was so far gone on drugs that the chances of him going straight were three million to one. "He was out of control," the psychiatrist said. "I don't think he would have lived much longer." Though Nat could have hospitalized him, he didn't. "You can't pin Johnny Cash down," he said.

Nat's plan was for Johnny not to be left alone while he detoxed. A "crew" gathered: June, Maybelle and Ezra Carter, Carl Perkins, Fluke Holland, and Braxton Dixon and his wife Anna. Each day during that October, Nat came by for a session with his patient. He scheduled drug withdrawal over ten days, directing June to dole out the pills in decreasing doses. Closed in his bedroom, Johnny didn't see or hear the pushers who rang the doorbell. When one of them wouldn't leave, Anna Dixon backed him down the driveway with a butcher knife.

Together, June, Maybelle, and Ezra did a lot of praying, and for Johnny, whose body was wracked with nausea, "every breath was a prayer, a fighting prayer." Though he wouldn't give up, he put his crew to the test. Yes, he assured Nat, he must never take drugs. But in the night, thrashing and fitful, he stalked his own hiding places. He tore cornices off drapes, yanked drawers from their tracks, ripped up carpet at doorways, unscrewed electrical plates. However, June and Braxton had been thorough. They had found enough pills to fill a cookie jar. Not a single demon remained in the house.

Withdrawing from tranquilizers was even harder

for Johnny than from amphetamines. He was beset with what he called "the ragin', screamin' terrors." He dreamed his stomach was filled with glass balls that pulled at him so hard, he felt his skin coming off. He was thrust up through trees and over the house. Then the balls broke into thousands of glass splinters that came alive, wriggling inside his arms and legs. When he awoke, he vowed that if he could just "hold out," he'd "get better." After three weeks, he did. He was hungry, sober, and gaining weight. One night, he asked June for frozen strawberries; he devoured two large packages with a quart of milk.

His first trip from the house was on a Sunday morning in November. June brought him to the Baptist church in Hendersonville. That evening, after two months off from performing, he gave a benefit show at Hendersonville High School so its band could buy uniforms to play at Miami's Orange Bowl. His final offering of the night, thrumming above the students like a chastened angel with a guitar, was a gospel song.

Johnny had survived his own hell on earth and had beaten the odds in less than a month. He confounded all the people who had predicted his death. But why not? He was, after all, one of a kind. He was Johnny Cash.

NINE

THE LAUGHTER OF six girls filled the Hendersonville house. With Johnny sober, and the divorce final, Vivian Cash had agreed to send Rosanne, Kathy, Cindy, and Tara to visit their father, and June had introduced them to her girls, twelve-year-old Carlene and nine-year-old Rosey. Johnny made popcorn in the big kitchen, cracking jokes and telling stories. He saw joy in his daughters' eyes; he didn't seem tired or sick to them now.

He knew that June's love for him, and his for her, had kept him afloat—though he'd had to swim the final depths by himself. Thwarting the yearning for drugs that he would have for the rest of his life, he and June began each day with a prayer. In February 1968, performing in Ontario, Canada, he turned to June

Performing with June Carter Cash at the Country Music Association Awards show in October 1977.

onstage and asked her to marry him. Shocked, she softly suggested, "Let's go on with the show," but the five thousand fans in the audience would not let her ignore the question. "Yes!" they shouted. "Say yes!" And, blushing, June finally replied, "Yes. Yes, I will."

The church wedding was performed March 1, 1968, in Franklin, Kentucky, just north of Nashville. The prediction that Johnny had made when he met June Carter—that they'd be married someday—had come true. Now he was thirty-six years old, and she was thirty-eight. At the reception, attended by hundreds of relatives and friends, the happy couple also celebrated their first Grammy together, a joint award for their single, "Jackson," in a Best Country and Western Performance category.

Johnny tried making amends to the people he had disappointed while he was on pills. He apologized to his parents, siblings, and children, and to Vivian, Maybelle, and Ezra; he thanked Saul Holiff for tolerating him, and offered concert impresarios every booking he had missed at his original fee (his current fee was much higher).

Nineteen sixty-eight was one of Johnny's busiest

years for concert tours. In early January, he had asked Columbia to take a big musical leap: to release an album of a live performance before hardened criminals at California's Folsom Prison. When the company hesitantly agreed, Floyd Gressett, who was Folsom's minister, secured the warden's permission, and electricians set up sound equipment in the dining hall of the prison. Johnny and his troupe appeared on January 13, 1968, in the groundbreaking music event. No entertainer had ever been professionally recorded performing in a prison environment.

Johnny's voice—searing, grave, honest—struck a nerve with Folsom inmates. He sang "Folsom Prison Blues," along with "Busted," a Harlan Howard song about a man unable to pay his bills or clothe his children; "I Got Stripes," a lament on daily prison life; "The Wall," about a convict's plan to escape or possibly to commit suicide by a guard's rifle; and "Green Grass of Home," a song about an inmate dreaming of going home who awakens to realize it's his execution day.

The audience at Folsom broke into wild applause, stomping feet, banging tables, and cheering for the Man in Black. Describing the event, author Dave

Urbanski said: "In short . . . [Johnny's] one of them. Part of the family. Close to the earth. Familiar with struggle."

When Columbia released *Johnny Cash at Folsom Prison*, it hit the top of the *Billboard* charts and sold a bombshell six million copies. Reviewer Chet Flippo said he thought it was the best live album ever produced. Johnny won a Grammy for the year's best album notes, which appeared in handwritten script on the back jacket cover. "You'll feel," he wrote about performing at Folsom, "the single pulsation of two thousand heartbeats in men who have had their hearts torn out, as well as their minds, their nervous systems, and their souls."

Following the album release, Johnny, June, and the rest of the troupe set off on a whirlwind tour of Europe, playing major concert halls. Thousands packed the streets to catch a glimpse of the man who had given country music such enormous urban popularity. After the European tour, with a Bible correspondence course packed in their suitcases, Johnny and June traveled by themselves to Israel, the first of several Holy Land trips, to see sacred sites.

On August 5, 1968, news came, however, that shocked musicians everywhere. Luther Perkins had died from burns and smoke inhalation in a house fire. For Johnny, part of his past vanished. Luther, who had once appeared at gigs with his secondhand, worn-out amplifier, had remained the unaffected good ole boy. At the funeral, Carl Perkins, Marshall, Johnny, and Fluke were pallbearers.

In January 1969, Johnny and June traveled to Vietnam to entertain the troops and visit wounded soldiers in army hospitals. Too little sleep and too much singing gave Johnny a high fever, but he didn't want to cancel the remaining shows. The doctor called to his hotel room, unaware of his patient's history, prescribed two dozen Dexedrine capsules, one to be taken each day. Within twenty-four hours, Johnny had swallowed a handful of pills and, alarming June, was "staggering and fumbling and mumbling." Mortified at himself, he flushed the rest of the Dexedrine down a toilet in Tokyo, his next stop after Vietnam.

In February, with his demons again banished, he gave a second live prison concert, this time at San Quentin, California's oldest maximum-security penitentiary. Because of his drug relapse, he felt an even deeper kinship with inmates who battled, as Johnny would write, their own "hounds of hell."

One thousand prisoners, some on death row, came to the concert in the prison mess hall. With the first guitar note he played, Johnny had the convicts on the edge of their seats. His "I Walk the Line" was faster and rougher than the original version. "Big River" and "Wreck of the Old '97" had a pulsing immediacy. Yells blasted the mess hall, egging Johnny on to joke about his own time behind bars. According to music reviewer Eamonn McCusker, Johnny told the inmates he was just a guy who'd happened to get lucky "with some chords, melodies, and lyrics."

Midway through his program, he sang "San Quentin," which he had written especially for the prisoners. Guards raised their rifles at the raucous response. The convicts, Johnny said, "were standing up on the dining tables. . . . All I had to do was say 'Break!' and they were gone. . . ."

San Quentin, you've been livin' hell to me.
You've galled at me since nineteen sixty-three.

I've seen 'em come and go and I've seen them die,
And long ago I stopped askin' why.

San Quentin, I hate ev'ry inch of you.
You've cut me and you've scarred me through an'
    through.
And I'll walk out a wiser, weaker man;
Mr. Congressman, why can't you understand?

San Quentin, what good do you think you do?
Do you think that I'll be different when you're
    through?
You bend my heart and mind and you warp my soul;
Your stone walls turn my blood a little cold.

San Quentin, may you rot and burn in hell.
May your walls fall and may I live to tell.
May all the world forget you ever stood.
And the whole world will regret you did no good.

San Quentin, you've been livin' hell to me.

Johnny Cash at San Quentin outsold the Folsom

album and won an unprecedented five Country Music Association awards. The most famous song to emerge from the concert was "A Boy Named Sue," by composer, author, and cartoonist Shel Silverstein. Off the cuff, since he hadn't rehearsed the lyrics, Johnny sang the song about a fellow wanting to kill the father who had abandoned him after naming him Sue. "Well," Johnny sang, "I grew up quick and I grew up mean, my fists got hard and my wits got keen, and I roamed from town to town to hide my shame." Father and son finally reunite, but at the song's end, the son claims if he ever has his own boy, he'll name him "Bill or George or any damn thing but Sue. I still hate that name!"

Near the end of the San Quentin show, Johnny spoke about his Christian faith. He described going to Israel with June and seeing the Wailing Wall and the Way of the Cross. Then he sang "He Turned the Water into Wine," and guards' mouths fell open at the sight of tough inmates openly weeping. No rifles were raised, not then and certainly not during Johnny's version of "Peace in the Valley," the gospel hymn sung at his brother Jack's funeral in 1944:

Well, the bear will be gentle and the wolf will be
   tame,
And the lion shall lie down with the lamb,
That's what it says,
And the beasts from the wild will be led by a child,
And I will be changed, changed from this creature
That I am, oh, yes.

Change was hard won—for Johnny, for the inmates, and for anyone fighting their own "hounds of hell"—but it was possible.

In 1969, *LIFE* magazine ran a feature article on "The Rough-Cut King of Country Music." "With . . . songs that may as well be fired from six-guns," wrote *LIFE*'s Alfred G. Arnowitz, "Johnny Cash has gone thundering through his career like a night-riding missionary . . . [with] a language that speaks to everyone." At Johnny's four-night booking at Albuquerque's New Mexico State Fair, one thousand people had to be turned away from his final show. By then, he had racked up more record album sales than any other American entertainer except Barbra Streisand and Johnny Mathis.

In 1970, he performed at the White House for President Nixon, and he spoke before a senate subcommittee hearing on prison reform. In 1971, he costarred with Kirk Douglas in the movie *A Gunfight*, financed by an Apache tribe grateful for Johnny's *Bitter Tears* album.

Producers at ABC-TV had approached Johnny about hosting a prime-time Saturday-night show, headlining musicians of his choice. He was wary of the white-shirt-and-tie guys, but he agreed that TV could bring him a new audience. *The Johnny Cash Show* ran from 1969 to 1971, fascinating viewers with its mixed-bag guest list: singers of folk, gospel, rock, pop, and country music, and various comedians and actors. Johnny did the show in Nashville, where he now felt most comfortable, hosting and singing from the Ryman Auditorium. He had refused California as home base, saying, "That's a whole different way of life out there. That's not where I want to be. That's not what I want to be."

After two years of exceptional TV ratings from his high-voltage songs, Johnny went back to talking, this time on camera, of his faith. The producers strongly objected but couldn't get him to stop. He was not trying to convert anyone, he said. But the millions of fans who admired his gospel songs and his earnest tale of "bad boy turned good" couldn't stop the ratings from falling, and *The Johnny Cash Show* was canceled. As for Johnny, he was glad to be free of the chaos of doing weekly TV.

Before he went off the air, Johnny introduced a new song—"The Man in Black"—on his show's second to last episode. He told viewers that black stood for all those excluded or sacrificed by society:

> *I wear the black for the poor and beaten down,*
> *Livin' in the homeless, hungry side of town,*
> *I wear it for the prisoner who has long paid for his*
>   *crime,*
> *But is there because he's a victim of the times. . . .*
>
> *Ah, I'd love to wear a rainbow every day,*
> *And tell the world that everything's OK,*
> *But I'll try to carry off a little darkness on my back;*
> *Till things are brighter, I'm the Man in Black.*

Two gifts had arrived for Johnny amid the commotion of songs, concerts, appearances, and his TV show. One, in 1970, was a telephone call from Reverend Billy Graham, America's leading religious revivalist. Reverend Graham hoped Johnny's renewal of faith could be a beacon to America's youth. The two men met and became friends, and Johnny and June went on to appear in amphitheaters at many of the Billy Graham worldwide crusades that converted thousands of people to believing in Jesus Christ. "Sometimes," Johnny would say about working with Reverend Graham, "I can be a signpost . . . sow a seed."

The second gift, delivered at Madison Hospital on March 3, 1970, was the birth of John Carter Cash. Johnny and June were thrilled over having a baby. Their immediate family now contained seven children. Intent on being a better father this time, Johnny even quit cigarettes when smoke made John Carter cough.

The following year, the Cashes took another trip to Israel. In this new phase of his life—married to June, father of a son, and not taking drugs—Johnny decided to produce a movie about the life of Jesus. He and June, with forty cast and crew members, obtained permission from the Israeli government to film the project. Johnny studied religious writers, biblical reference books, and filmmaking, slept only three hours a night, and narrated the movie he called *Gospel Road*. Songs he wrote carried the story line, as did material from other musicians like John Denver and Kris Kristofferson.

Twentieth Century Fox funded *Gospel Road* in its early release days, but few movie theaters rented it. Johnny promoted the movie wherever he toured, and after a year, Billy Graham's World Wide Pictures distributed it. Hundreds of churches, as well as movie houses, now showed the film, and missionaries used it in Africa and India. Johnny and June had invested $500,000 in the movie, but profits went to charity.

Back home in Hendersonville, Johnny took two-year-old John Carter to watch the fish jumping in Old Hickory Lake and to visit Ray and Carrie, who had moved across the road. He and June bought a nearby farm, Bon Aqua, and a redbrick house as a business office for tour schedules, bookings (through Johnny's latest and last manager, Lou Robin), and music publishing. The Cash family had stayed in close contact. Roy often visited Johnny, and Reba relocated to manage the Hendersonville office and its tourist attractions, a small Cash museum and a souvenir shop.

On his acres of land, Johnny planted tomatoes, fig bushes, roses, and grapevines, and brought in wild boar, ostriches, and buffalo. In an old log cabin, which he eventually turned into a recording studio, he spent hours reading, drawing, creating songs, and writing his first autobiography, *The Man in Black*, published in 1975. The book, submitted in longhand to Zondervan Publishing House, sold over a million copies. It was a frank, gripping tale of his life.

This new, more stable phase in Johnny's life was not, however, risk-free. Johnny and June traveled with John Carter who, at three years old, stood onstage next to his father and sang "Mary Had a Little Lamb." Once, someone threw a rock at a limousine carrying the family and shattered a window. Kidnap threats were also made against John Carter. An extortion note warned: "Johnny Cash if you want to keep making money and keep your family healthy leave $200,000 in old bills in a plastic bag at interstate 24 at Old Hickory

Boulevard Friday night." The Cashes notified the police and hired security guards.

Tourists on foot, in cars, or in chartered buses arrived by the thousands at Johnny's house. Five hundred cars passed by on Saturday afternoons, even more on Sundays. Johnny chatted with fans who said they had driven across the country to see him. But when he found a stranger in the bedroom of June's daughter Rosey, he dragged the man downstairs and threw him out. In spite of all this, he felt gratitude toward his fans. Their attendance at his performances kept him singing all over the world. He shook their hands, signed autographs, and let his photo be taken. He donated to many charities, large and small. When he heard about an indigent man in Nashville with kidney disease, he paid for a lifesaving dialysis machine.

Looking for some privacy, Johnny and June purchased a home in Montego Bay, Jamaica, in 1976. Cinnamon Hill, built in 1747 on a cliff 280 feet above sea level, had first belonged to the family of poet Elizabeth Barrett Browning. The house was a refuge for the Cashes, but on December 21, 1981, it became a place of horror. June, Johnny, and John Carter were having dinner with several friends and family members when three men burst in with stockings over their heads. Brandishing a knife, a machete, and a gun, they threatened to kill John Carter if they weren't paid one million dollars.

Johnny said at once that he didn't keep much money in Jamaica, so the men ransacked the house, stealing valuables. They held the gun to John Carter's head, yanked June by the hair, and demanded that everyone lie on the floor. Savvy about trigger-happy criminals, Johnny controlled his rage, and after four terrible hours the men locked their hostages in the basement and escaped in June's Land Rover.

Johnny and his guests battered down the basement door with a coat tree and called the police. Two of the thieves were quickly caught at the airport (they were later killed during a jail break), and the third, located sixteen days after the crime, was shot dead while resisting arrest.

Jamaica's prime minister, Edward Seaga, apologized in person to Johnny for the torment his family suffered at Cinnamon Hill. Yet Johnny, well aware of the risks of celebrity, held no ill will toward Jamaica. Fame had sent him a frightening downer, but scarcely a week later, it provided an upper as well. On January 9, 1982, after he had returned with June and John Carter to Tennessee, a five-mile stretch of Gallatin Road in Hendersonville was renamed Johnny Cash Parkway. The South that Johnny had loved all his life, singing its praises on records and in concerts, was singing back to him.

Johnny held the microphone for three-year-old John Carter Cash while he sang "Mary Had a Little Lamb," May 1, 1973.

TEN

THE LATE 1970S and the 1980s brought hard times to country music. Though Johnny's concerts still sold out, his new record releases had low sales. Teenage music buyers were listening to punk rock, rap, hip-hop, and rock 'n' roll. New stars like Michael Jackson, Madonna, and Guns N' Roses emerged. Johnny could see that music was more often born now in corporate boardrooms than in the hearts of artists.

He went fishing with his friend Bob Dylan off the Hendersonville dock and gave him his favorite Martin guitar. In 1968, following Dylan's prophetic hit song "The Times They Are A-Changin'," they had written a song together, "Wanted Man." On the dock, they agreed they were both doing their "thing" in a rapidly shifting music world.

Johnny was also watching his children change.

Rosanne had graduated from high school in 1973 and, moving in with her father and June, began a singing/songwriting career. She went on to score many country hits in the 1980s, including a cover of her father's "Tennessee Flat Top Box," which went to #1. Cindy Cash and June's daughters Carlene and Rosey also sang professionally, and all four women performed regularly with Johnny and his troupe. Kathy Cash, at eighteen, worked at the Hendersonville office, House of Cash; Tara Cash wanted to act; and John Carter already had an ear for music.

A huge loss for the Cashes and for the music industry came in October 22, 1978, with the death of Maybelle Carter. Johnny often said that Maybelle's support helped save his life during many of his drug binges. She was buried in Hendersonville cemetery, her many friends and relatives singing "Will the Circle Be Unbroken" at her gravesite.

In 1980, the Cash family found comfort when Johnny was inducted into the Country Music Hall of Fame, the youngest living person to receive this honor. Because of its roots in Southern music, the award meant more to him than any others he received. In his acceptance speech, he advised musicians to keep an independent style. "Do it your way," he said. "Don't let yourself get caught in a bag."

His own style had involved an intriguing contrast of brooding gravity, wry humor, and defiance. He recorded a religious album for Columbia, *The Holy Land*, produced in Israel and dedicated to Jack, but he performed annually for hard drinkers and gamblers at a Las Vegas hotel. He bantered with the high-rolling crowd, but in his gospel segment he had the face of Jesus projected onto a huge backdrop. And he got away with it. He sang lyrics like "Early one morning, while making the rounds, I took a shot of cocaine, and I shot my woman down" ("Cocaine Blues"), yet maintained his close friendship with Billy Graham. In 1976, his #1 hit was "One Piece at a Time," a quirky ballad about an automobile worker who steals parts from an assembly line to build himself a car.

In an effort to stay on top of marketing its music, Columbia had persuaded Johnny to record an album of songs chosen by outside producers. The 1974 result, *John R. Cash*, was a dull concoction of lyrics that just didn't have the Johnny Cash verve. He took matters into his own hands for *Rockabilly Blues* and *Johnny 99*. Released in 1980 and 1983, respectively, both albums had the Cash growl and edge. He also recorded *Highwayman*, an album collaboration with Willie Nelson, Waylon Jennings, and Kris Kristofferson, his first #1 hit of the decade. The four craggy-faced singers had, according to author Michael McCall, "survived 12 marriages, more than 115 years on the road and an endless amount of whiskey and pills." Fortunately, they had outlasted the "bad old days" and came together to make a historic album.

In 1983, a freak accident put Johnny in the hospital. A normally friendly ostrich named Waldo lived on his Hendersonville property. The bird had lost its mate in a winter freeze and, one icy day, seeing Johnny nearby, it advanced angrily. Johnny grabbed a stick, but Waldo struck out with one foot, hitting him in the stomach, splitting open skin, and breaking two of his ribs. When he fell, Johnny crashed onto a rock and broke two other ribs.

In the hospital emergency room, his ribs were taped and he was given a bottle of pain pills. Less than two weeks later, on a twelve-stop tour in Nottingham,

England, Johnny was hallucinating from the pills. Pacing a hotel room, he told June that a pull-down Murphy bed was behind the wall paneling, and he tore at the panels, piercing his right hand with splinters. "When I got home," he said, "my hand was just a giant ball of infection, so I had to check into Baptist Hospital and have surgery on it." Unfortunately, he hid some pills in a tobacco sack and tied it behind the hospital TV set. After his hand surgery, doctors had to operate again because he had developed unrelated abdominal bleeding; his duodenum and part of his spleen, stomach, and intestines were removed.

Recuperating, Johnny retrieved his tobacco sack and hid the pills under the bandages covering his fresh incision. "I thought I'd been really clever," he said. But the pills slowly dissolved into his wound, and as they combined with the morphine he was receiving, he lapsed into a coma. His hidden stash was only discovered because he woke up long enough to mumble to his doctor about checking the bandages. Even after finding the pills, though, the staff continued the morphine shots. "They didn't know who they were dealing with," Johnny said, "or what: more dope just made me more crazy."

Cash family members, along with Johnny's troupe and technicians on his payroll, were aghast at his latest drug debacle. Filing into the hospital room, they read aloud letters they had written to him about betrayal, fear, lies, and broken trust. The saddest moment for Johnny was when thirteen-year-old John Carter, who deeply loved his father, spoke tearfully of embarrassment in front of his friends. The group at his bedside asked Johnny to enter Betty Ford Center, a substance-abuse clinic in Rancho Mirage, California. He didn't fight the idea.

He spent forty-three days at the Center, living in a dormitory, following a twelve-step program, and meeting daily with a counselor. He exercised and ate healthy food. During Family Week, his manager Lou Robin, agent Marty Klein, and June and John Carter joined some of his sessions. He talked of a family vulnerability to drugs that had struck two of his sisters, two of his brothers, and all four of his daughters. But now that he was clean again, he saw that a fall didn't mean failure. He would have "an ongoing struggle," but he could get help.

Back on track, Johnny collaborated on another Highwayman album. He had already taken cameo roles in *Little House on the Prairie*, *The Muppet Show*, and *Columbo*, and received high praise for his 1981 performance in CBS-TV's movie about adult illiteracy, *The Pride of Jessi Hallam*. Later he would appear in *Davy Crockett* and *Dr. Quinn, Medicine Woman*. In 1984, he and three former cohorts from the Sun Records days—Carl Perkins, Roy Orbison, and Jerry Lee Lewis—convened in Memphis to cut a *Class of '55* album.

At the rousing Memphis reunion, the Class of '55 sang Johnny's "Hey, Porter," "Folsom Prison," and "I Walk the Line"; Carl's "Blue Suede Shoes"; Jerry Lee's "Whole Lotta Shakin' Goin' On"; and Roy's "Ooby Dooby." These songs were like homing pigeons set into flight, bringing messages and memories to devoted listeners.

In 1985, at eighty-eight years old and nearly blind, Ray Cash died. Johnny's three oldest daughters had already married and divorced. Half a century had passed since Johnny had watched his father wielding a long-handled machete on Dyess land, or heard him calling out for Johnny to shut off the Sears Roebuck radio. When Johnny was famous, Ray had come as often as possible to hear his son sing.

After his father's death, prodded and encouraged by Billy Graham, Johnny finished writing a novel about St. Paul the Apostle. He focused on Paul's radiant vision on the road to Damascus. Paul had endured great trials of faith—being "shipwrecked, beaten with rods, thrown in boiling oil, snake-bitten, stoned, and left for dead"—but found peace in every situation. "I wanted some of that [peace]," Johnny said.

The novel, *Man in White*, was completed at Bon Aqua farm and published in 1986 by Harper & Row. In it, as in *Gospel Road*, Johnny had made a major effort to set forth his spiritual beliefs. He dedicated *Man in White* "to my father, RAY CASH / 1897–1985 / Veteran of World War I / Discharge: Honorable / Conduct: Good."

Following a book tour, Johnny's Columbia contract came up for renewal. In a move that flabbergasted the industry, the CBS-owned corporation announced it was dropping him. Music producers and agents stormed

Columbia's offices, reminding studio executives that for twenty-eight years Johnny Cash had provided a huge chunk of the corporation's profits. Columbia's decision, however, was final. Johnny was a megastar, but fast-changing music styles and trends had affected his sales. Record companies were now signing up younger country singers like Randy Travis, Reba McEntire, and Ricky Skaggs.

Johnny never could stomach the corporate game. He rarely attended Columbia meetings and avoided their lawyers and accountants. Much of the current music sounded the same to him; he wanted to sing what he liked, the way he wanted to sing it. He might miss his busy recording years at Columbia, but he'd strum his guitar someplace else. As Florida State University Professor David Kirby wrote, "Johnny Cash didn't have to be who anyone else wanted him to be."

Other music companies courted Johnny, and he signed with Mercury/Polygram. In 1987 and 1988, they released the albums *Johnny Cash Is Coming to Town* and *Water from the Wells of Home*. For the latter album, he composed the title track with John Carter and sang a duet with June. One song, "New Moon over Jamaica," was written especially for Johnny by Paul McCartney of the Beatles.

Mercury's promotion of Johnny's albums proved to be lax. Country radio had been ignoring the older stars, so Mercury, like Columbia, hyped its young performers. Even though rock fans enjoyed Johnny's performance at the Ritz, a New York club, and watched his TV appearance on *Saturday Night Live*, the five albums he recorded for Mercury sold a total of only 200,000 copies.

Frustrated by the cartloads of albums sitting in company warehouses, Johnny perked up when, in 1988, the Country Music Hall of Fame opened a Johnny Cash exhibit. Featuring photographs, posters, concert outfits worn by the Man in Black, film from his early TV appearances, guitars, and other memorabilia, the exhibit attracted over one million people during the two years it was open.

The late 1980s were marked by new worries over Johnny's health. In May 1987, at a concert in Council Bluffs, Iowa, his speech slurred. June took him to a hospital where doctors diagnosed an irregular heartbeat. Almost a year later, he was hospitalized in

Palm Springs, California, for bronchitis and laryngitis. And at the end of 1988, twelve days before Christmas, he was visiting Waylon Jennings, who had undergone bypass heart surgery, when Waylon's doctors suggested Johnny have medical tests. The results showed a 90 percent blockage at the fork of two coronary arteries. He was admitted to Baptist Hospital the next morning for immediate surgery.

The procedure began at eight A.M. and lasted two hours. Back in his room, Johnny was in extreme pain, his heart blockage having been bypassed with blood vessels from his chest and leg. Waylon Jennings had assured him the surgery was a piece of cake, but later admitted he was lying so that Johnny wouldn't fly the coop. Doctors juggled post-surgery medications and, for several days, he seemed stabilized. Then pneumonia set in, and he was gravely ill.

Advised that her husband might die, a distraught June called family members and asked Lou Robin to fly in on Christmas Day. Newspaper reporters scrambled to prepare obituaries. In Johnny's version of the crisis, he heard nurses shouting, "He's slipping! He's slipping!" Then he saw a light described by many patients in near-death experiences. St. Paul the Apostle, the subject of Johnny's *Man in White*, had witnessed a similar brightness.

Though Johnny didn't want to leave his beloved June, his family, or his songs still to be sung, the light was euphoric to him. When his pulse grew stronger on its own, and he realized he wasn't "on the other side," and that part of him longed to be there, he yanked at the tubes connecting him to life-saving equipment. It was June who calmed him down, holding his hand as Christmas bells rang out in the corridor.

A local disk jockey had constructed a huge Christmas/Get Well card beneath his hospital room window, signed by four thousand fans. By New Year's Day 1989, Johnny did not want to be anywhere except on earth. He had his music, he had his family, and he had his defiant spirit back—in spades. "When death starts beating the door down," he'd say, "you need to be reaching for your shotgun."

ELEVEN

OUT OF THE BLUE, in 1993, a man barely thirty years old, with a beard down to his chest and a record company steeped in rap, hip-hop, and heavy metal, walked into Johnny's life. Rick Rubin's Def American Records had a lineup of young rebel artists that kept censors busy, including the Beastie Boys, Red Hot Chili Peppers, Run DMC, and Andrew Dice Clay. Rick told Johnny that he wanted to record him.

Johnny just smiled. He was, after all, sixty-two years old, with a penchant for gospel, not rap. But the two men arranged to talk at a restaurant in Santa Ana, California, before one of Johnny's concerts. "I have always been drawn," Rubin said later, "to things that are edgy and extreme. Johnny Cash was . . . an outsider, and I think that's what drew me to him more than anything else."

What Rick offered Johnny was irresistible to him:

to sing or tape anything and everything he wanted, accompanied only by his guitar, in the comfort of Rick's Los Angeles home. No corporate pressure. No board meetings.

Lou Robin negotiated for Rick to buy out the Mercury contract, and though Johnny was busy touring with the Highwaymen and appearing at the Wayne Newton Theatre in Branson, Missouri, he loved recording for Rick. They taped ninety-four songs in Rick's living room and his log-cabin studio. The power of Johnny Cash singing alone was unmistakable. Rick booked him into the Viper Room, a hip West Hollywood nightclub co-owned by movie star Johnny Depp.

Johnny was apprehensive about connecting solo—with none of the backup singers, drums, or guitars he had used for thirty years—with a "cool" young crowd. But midway through the song "Delia's Gone" (about a man who kills his unfaithful girlfriend), the normally noisy crowd fell silent. None of them had been born when "I Walk the Line" first throbbed on the airwaves, but they knew about Johnny's outlaw status, his drug busts, and his meltdowns. Now they heard his commanding voice. The next day's newspapers crowed over his impact on young people. Headlines read: "Johnny Cash, Austerely Direct from Deep Within," "Cash Conquers," "Chordless in Gaza: The Second Coming of John R. Cash," and "Johnny Cash: American Music Legend."

Johnny cemented his connection to fans of alternative music when he recorded singer/songwriter Bono's "The Wanderer" for the U2 band's album *Zooropa*. In late 1993, *Zooropa* hit #1 in both Britain and the U.S., selling over seven million copies worldwide. The next April, Rick Rubin released Johnny's album, *American Recordings*, a blood-stirring song journey into bondage, freedom, loneliness, and sorrow. *The New York Times* said Johnny's "tales of darkness and doubt are not dead ends, but thorough-fares in the struggle that is life." *Rolling Stone* gave the album five stars. "John Cash," Rick Rubin said, "is real. In show business—or call it art, to con the suckers—in any racket, alternative or not, that is the rarest metal of all."

Three major Johnny Cash/Rick Rubin albums followed *American Recordings: Unchained* in 1996, for which Johnny wrote the song "Meet Me in Heaven," the phrase inscribed on Jack's and his father's headstones; *Solitary Man* in 2000; and *The Man Comes Around* in 2002. Johnny thought the albums were his best work since the 1950s, and reviewers agreed. Referring to his chilling cover of Nick Cave's "The Mercy Seat" on *Solitary Man* (about a convict awaiting execution), journalist Terry Staunton said, "It is one of the most astonishing pieces of music ever recorded." To *Vogue* magazine's Richard Goldstein, Johnny's tales of struggle transformed everything he sang "into what you feel when you're alone in a room." With Rick Rubin's input, Johnny's aging record career was reborn.

Johnny respected the energy, rebellion, and truth-seeking of young listeners who sent him positive vibes. He received awards reflecting his appeal to a new generation of fans, including his induction into the Rock and Roll Hall of Fame. Johnny is the only musician officially installed in three halls of fame (Country Music, Rock and Roll, and Songwriters). In 1994, he appeared at Carnegie Hall with Rosanne, and in 1996 he was honored by the John F. Kennedy Center for the Performing Arts. That same year, he was awarded a Grammy for Best Country Album for *Unchained*. In

1999, he received Lifetime Achievement Awards from the Grammy Awards, and another Grammy in 2000 for *Solitary Man*. So much was happening in his sixties that, in 1997, he wrote his second autobiography, *Cash: The Autobiography*, with journalist Patrick Carr.

By 1997, having fought chronic pain from surgeries on an old jawbone break, Johnny sometimes shook uncontrollably—but not from pills. After a nine-country European tour, he and June reduced his schedule. That summer, he found himself involuntarily walking backwards on New York's Madison Avenue, and at an October concert in Flint, Michigan, he bent to retrieve a guitar pick and toppled toward the floor. He told the audience, who assumed he was joking, that he had Parkinson's Disease. He didn't, but tests showed he had autonomic neuropathy, an incurable nervous-system disorder. He would never let himself stop composing, singing, or working with Rick Rubin, but Flint, Michigan, was his last concert.

"He's faced a lot of challenges in his life," Lou Robin told the press about Johnny's illness. "He thrives on challenges." However, on October 29, 1997, he was hospitalized with a devastating combination of nerve damage, diabetes, and pneumonia. His body, assailed for so many years by drugs, seemed to collapse all at once. He fell into a twelve-day coma, with June and his family praying by his side. Not able to quite wake up, he remembered trying to proclaim, "I'm *not* dying."

When the coma lifted, Johnny was visited by his friend, country star Merle Haggard, who was once an inmate at San Quentin for attempted robbery. On the liner notes in Merle's 1999 album *For the Record*, Johnny wrote about Merle leaning over him in the hospital and gripping him hard—like he was afraid he would have to let go. Barely opening his eyes, Johnny had mumbled, "Is that you, Hag?" Merle nodded his head. Visitors were allowed to stay only one minute, but in that dark and dangerous fight for survival, Johnny knew Merle Haggard's heartfelt one minute with him was precious beyond measure.

In the mid-1990s, Johnny took a trip back to Dyess, his first since 1968. He stood in the fields where, as a boy, he stuffed cotton bolls into sacks. The old house was crumbling, but he smelled the peanuts he and Jack had roasted and sold for ten cents a bag at the movie theater. When Dyess High School burned down in the 1960s, Johnny had donated money to help replace it, and a plaque in Jack's memory was mounted at the shop where he had died. Jack's death still seemed like yesterday to Johnny.

In 2000, he was back in the hospital with pneumonia, the fourth time in three years. He had developed asthma, digestive problems, and glaucoma. His neurological disorder made walking difficult. He never complained, however. He saw his afflictions as a test of faith and resolve. His voice sometimes wavered but it kept its brooding dignity. When he recorded musician Tom Petty's "I Won't Back Down," he meant every word he sang.

Residents of Nashville, fearful now of losing their ill, renegade star, turned out by the thousands for a 2002 Johnny Cash tribute at Ryman Auditorium. Turner Network Television also toasted him in New York, with actor Jon Voight as MC and songs and tributes given by June, Kris Kristofferson, Sheryl Crow, Trisha Yearwood, Bob Dylan, Lyle Lovett, U2, Bruce Springsteen, and others.

Johnny wasn't sure he could make it to New York,

but at the last minute, using June's favorite expression, he decided to "press on." Ensconced backstage at the Hammerstein Ballroom, he waited through a spine-tingling ensemble rendition of his old gospel song "Belshazzar" and through June's version, with guitar, fiddle, and autoharp, of "Ring of Fire." Then he came onstage, his black guitar strapped on his back. His body was weak, bent from the shoulders, but when the spotlight hit him, he looked ramrod straight. Applause exploded like a bomb.

Illness was never as daunting to Johnny as the growing list of people he had lost: Jack, his parents, and Maybelle; Anita Carter, Helen Carter, Roy Orbison, Carl Lewis, and most recently, Waylon Jennings. Nothing prepared him, however, for May 2003. June had heart-valve surgery and seemed to be rallying when she suddenly went into cardiac arrest. An anguished Johnny sat beside her respirator, talking to her, pleading with her not to leave. In a song they had recorded in the 1970s, "Far-Side Banks of Jordan," they pledged that whoever died first would await the other at the desert kingdom, rising up with a shout at the sight of the beloved, wading through shallow water with an outreached hand. And on May 15, at 5:04 P.M., June

Carter Cash—the woman whom Johnny called "my rock, my anchor"—died at age seventy-three.

John Carter sadly expressed what it meant for his father to lose June. "The two were one," he said. "When she left, part of him just wasn't there anymore." At the funeral, Johnny was helped out of a wheelchair so he could stand by the coffin and say good-bye. Rosanne delivered the eulogy, explaining that, for June, there "were two kinds of people—those she knew and loved, and those she didn't know and loved." Later, at a family gathering, Johnny said his grief was "so severe, there is no way of describing it."

From then on, he slept in his small office at the house. Because of his glaucoma, he could no longer read the books lining the walls, but his children and grandchildren surrounded him. John Carter's daughter, Anna Maybelle, would curl up in his lap. He "talked" every day on the phone with June, as if she were listening at the other end. On the door of the electric elevator that brought his wheelchair (now a permanent fixture) from one floor to another, he had her portrait painted.

He also went back to work. It was, he said, what June wanted. In quiet discussions, he, Rick Rubin, and

John Carter planned a boxed set of CDs, *Unearthed*, for his many unreleased songs. Columbia, capitalizing on his "second coming" with Rick, had rereleased its Cash classics in a CD theme set, *Love, God, and Murder*, and a CD retrospective, *Man in Black—The Very Best of Johnny Cash*. Fox 2000 Pictures, with Johnny's agreement, began production on a movie of his life, *Walk the Line*.

Johnny's fourth Rick Rubin album, *The Man Comes Around*, had been released six months before June's death. He had worked hard on the title song, a soulful portent of Judgment Day. Among old standards on the album, like "Bridge Over Troubled Water" and "Desperado," is the last track, "We'll Meet Again," perhaps Johnny's farewell song to his fans. But the second track, "Hurt," written by Trent Reznor of Nine Inch Nails, is most harrowing, a tale of a life ravaged by drugs. The video of "Hurt," filmed in Johnny's Hendersonville home, shows him at seventy—white-haired and puffy-faced—half singing, half speaking the words while clips of him in his prime fly by like beautiful ghosts. The frailty in his voice only underscores his strength of spirit. "Cash flat out immortalizes 'Hurt,'" wrote author Dave Urbanski. "A century from now, [his] version will stand as the definitive interpretation."

I hurt myself today
To see if I still feel.
I focus on the pain,
The only thing that's real.

The needle tears a hole,
The old familiar sting.
Try to kill it all away,
But I remember everything.

Chorus:
What have I become?
My sweetest friend,
Everyone I know goes away
In the end.

And you could have it all,
My empire of dirt.
I will let you down;
I will make you hurt.

The name leading the 2003 list of nominees for MTV's Video Music Awards was Johnny Cash, the oldest nominee in MTV's history. His "Hurt" video won the award for cinematography, and at the August 28 ceremony he was saluted by pop star Justin Timberlake and rapper Snoop Dogg. Johnny had hoped to attend the event, but pancreatitis put him back in the hospital. He assured John Carter and his sister Joanne that he wasn't afraid of death; he had laid down his "shotgun" now. June and Jack and so many others awaited him, and he had made peace with old guilts and regrets. He knew God had forgiven him his sins, so he figured he might as well forgive himself.

Discharged from the hospital on September 9, he went home to Hendersonville, arranging with Rick Rubin by phone to go the next week to Los Angeles. But it was not to be. The last song he recorded, with John Carter as producer in the cabin studio, was "Engine 148," about an engineer's lament and death. On Thursday, September 11, Johnny had trouble breathing and was coughing up blood. Taken by ambulance to Baptist Hospital, he was met there by John Carter, Rosanne, and Kathy.

For over a decade, throughout all his illnesses, Johnny chose grace over misery, and purpose over despair. His dignity never left him in the last days of his life. At two A.M. on September 12, 2003, four months after June's death, the Man in Black, the quintessential outsider with the staggering voice, the occasional chip on his shoulder, and enough songs to wear out a guitar, was dead.

Over 1,500 people crowded into the private funeral at Hendersonville's First Baptist Church. Emmylou Harris and Sheryl Crow sang "The Old Rugged Cross" and Bob Dylan's "Every Grain of Sand." Franklin Graham, Billy's son, stood in for his father. Johnny was buried next to June in Hendersonville Memory Gardens, near Maybelle, Ezra, and Anita Carter. A black granite bench would grace Johnny's gravesite inscribed with CASH—CARTER and the two song titles most associated with Johnny and June: I WALK THE LINE and WILDWOOD FLOWER. In Nashville and New York, Johnny was honored in star-studded tributes, and 2003 and 2006 CD sets, *Unearthed* and *American V: A Hundred Highways*, respectively, which contained dozens of previously unreleased tracks, made him one of the most prolific posthumous song artists. Plans are also under way for Rick Rubin to release *American VI.*

The *New York Times* obituary for Johnny said he "was the vocal bedrock of American country music for more than four decades." *Country Music* magazine said "[he] strengthened the bonds between folk and country music so that both sides saw their similarities as well as their differences. He helped to liberalize Nashville so that it could accept the unconventional and the controversial. . . ."

Bono of U2 described Johnny as "more than wise. In a garden full of weeds—the oak tree." "He was a deeply spiritual man," said Kris Kristofferson, "a compassionate man willing and able to champion the voiceless and the underdog who was also something of a holy terror: Abraham Lincoln with a wild side." And according to Australian singer Nick Cave, "he had such a wealth of experience in his voice, heaven and hell and no one could touch him."

Johnny would have been proud that many singer/songwriters and their bands now express independence from the corporate grip. These non-mainstream groups flourish with relentless touring and fierce dedication to music. Johnny's work on behalf of prison reform and American Indians continues to spark change. Prisons and overall prison procedures are improved through community awareness; the Prison Reform Trust in England issues a quarterly magazine, *Prison Report*. In Washington, D.C., the National Museum of the American Indian opened in 2004, fostering greater understanding of Indian culture and hopes of reconciling a tragic Indian past.

The world may always remember Johnny Cash as the Arkansas child picking cotton in America's Depression who grew up to be an internationally famous singer. He wrote 1,500 songs, hitting *Billboard*'s Country Charts 137 times (52 of his songs made the Top Ten). He recorded nearly seventy albums and won eleven Grammys. For Johnny, however, his family was his greatest prize. Drug-free, he became the father and husband he wanted to be. He reveled in the successes and stood by in the struggles of six daughters, his son, and his grandchildren. Rosanne became an award-winning singer/songwriter/author who lives in New York and has five children; Kathy lives in Hendersonville and is raising three children; Cindy, an antique dealer, lives in Jackson, Mississippi, and has a daughter; Tara, a jewelry designer, lives in Portland, Oregon, and has two sons; and John Carter, a musician and record producer, lives in Hendersonville and has two children. June's daughter Carlene is a professional musician, but tragically, June's other daughter, Rosey, died of carbon-monoxide poisoning in October 2003.

Even as his life was singing its final chorus, music was Johnny Cash's infallible truth, his earthly gospel. We no longer see him striding onstage, his guitar slung over his shoulder, but we still have his voice. It grabs at us from our iPods, CDs, radios, and TVs—sometimes raw and shuddering, but always on the mark. That voice, sawing down our hardest edges, is an outlaw's stark and redemptive hymn. It can yank us to our feet or slam us, awestruck, to our knees. Listen. Just listen.

A special tribute to Johnny was included in the 2003 Country Music Association Awards show in Nashville, Tennessee.

SOURCE NOTES

INTRODUCTION

"I don't pretend . . .": Streissguth, *Ring of Fire*, 60.

"He was a poet . . .": Editors of Rolling Stone, *Cash*, 13.

CHAPTER ONE

"bare-bones . . . three . . .": Cash with Carr, *Cash*, 18.

"it all sounded . . .": Cash with Carr, *Cash*, 20.

"thick black Arkansas . . .": Cash with Carr, *Cash*, 20.

"protector; I was . . .": Cash, *Man in Black*, 30.

"real jungle" and "We've got some . . .": Cash with Carr, *Cash*, 21.

"Why? Why?": Wren, *Winners Got Scars Too*, 60.

reels and jigs: Dolan, *Johnny Cash*, 54.

"You've got infantile . . .": Cash, *Man in Black*, 67.

"Sometimes," "when you . . ." and "I sang through . . .": Cash, *Man in Black*, 67.

CHAPTER TWO

"A man dying alone . . .": Cash, *Man in Black*, 67.

Eddie Hill and . . . : Cash with Carr, *Cash*, 49.

"fake stuff": Cash with Carr, *Cash*, 68.

"You'll never do . . .": Cash with Carr, *Cash*, 69.

"You won't want . . .": Cash, *Man in Black*, 28.

"Turn that radio . . .": Wren, *Winners Got Scars Too*, 61.

"Come to God! . . .": Cash, *Man in Black*, 22.

"Hallelujah! Praise God! . . .": Cash, *Man in Black*, 22.

"didn't understand it . . .": Cash, *Man in Black*, 21.

"No two boys . . .": Cash, *Man in Black*, 27.

"twitchy and nervous": Cash, *Man in Black*, 33.

"spiritual accountability": Cash, *Man in Black*, 34.

"I really had . . .": Cash, *Man in Black*, 35.

"You're going to . . .": Cash, *Man in Black*, 41.

"No, son, I . . .": Cash with Carr, *Cash*, 35.

"I wish you . . ." "They're so beautiful . . ." and "He had intestinal . . .":
    Cash with Carr, *Cash*, 36.

"no way around . . .": Cash with Carr, *Cash*, 36.

"Which is Jack's . . .": Cash with Carr, *Cash*, 38.

CHAPTER THREE

"Who was that . . .": Cash, *Man in Black*, 56.

"That was me,": Cash, *Man in Black*, 56.

"God has His . . .": Cash with Carr, *Cash*, 72.

"Are they good . . .": Cash, *Man in Black*, 51.

"He remembered me!": Cash, *Man in Black*, 52.

"I'll be up there someday . . .": Cash, *Man in Black*, 51.

"Be a live wire . . .": Miller, S., *Johnny Cash*, 257.

"You're not gonna . . .": Wren, *Winners Got Scars Too*, 75.

"I was proud . . .": Wren, *Winners Got Scars Too*, 78.

"the right way . . .": Urbanski, *The Man Comes Around*, 8.

"only real [military] fight": Wren, *Winners Got Scars Too*, 80.

CHAPTER FOUR

"I saw him . . .": Wren, *Winners Got Scars Too*, 88.

"didn't run with . . .": Cash with Carr, *Cash*, 107.

"was tearing up . . .": Cash with Carr, *Cash*, 95.

"Mr. Phillips, sir . . . ": Cash with Carr, *Cash*, 101.

"Come back tomorrow . . . ": Cash with Carr, *Cash*, 102.

"sounded awful": Cash with Carr, *Cash*, 102.

"weeper": Cash with Carr, *Cash*, 102.

"A star, and . . .": Miller, S., *Johnny Cash*, 52.

"We're going to . . .": Cash, *Man in Black*, 102.

CHAPTER FIVE

"I couldn't believe . . .": Tosches, "Chordless in Gaza," *Ring of Fire*, 238.

"How do I . . .": Cash, *Man in Black*, 75.

"Mighty spiffy.": Cash, *Man in Black*, 75.

"Just don't step . . .": Cash, *Man in Black*, 75.

"sparse, no-frills": Urbanski, *The Man Comes Around*, 39.

"Even at age . . .": Editors of *Rolling Stone*, *Cash*, 32.

"He just melts . . .": Dearmore, "First Angry Man of Country Singers," in *New York Times Magazine*, 32.

"likely target appeared . . .": Campbell, *Johnny Cash*, 85.

"originate[d] in his . . .": Editors of *Rolling Stone*, *Cash*, 13.

"The more the world . . .": Cash, *Man in Black*, 76.

"I ought to . . .": Cash, *Man in Black*, 78.

"farmer food": Cash with Carr, *Cash*, 195.

"He learned how . . .": Wren, *Winners Got Scars Too*, 99.

"It was a wonder . . .": Carr, "Cash Comes Back," in *Ring of Fire*, 181.

"What makes you . . .": Carr, "Cash Comes Back," 181.

"Well . . . I love . . .": Carr, "Cash Comes Back," 182.

"The boy had . . .": *Nashville Banner* review.

"Take one of . . .": Cash, *Man in Black*, 81.

"What are they?": Cash, *Man in Black*, 81.

"Bennies,": Cash, *Man in Black*, 81.

"Will they hurt . . .": Cash, *Man in Black*, 81.

"Here . . . have one . . .": Cash, *Man in Black*, 81.

"at no extra . . .": Cash, *Man in Black*, 82.

"demon called Deception": Cash, *Man in Black*, 82.

CHAPTER SIX

"Luther? Don't worry . . .": Miller, S., *Johnny Cash*, 73.

"She saw them . . .": Cash with Carr, *Cash*, 196.

"soul, fire, and . . .": Cash with Carr, *Cash*, 108.

"I don't know . . .": Cash with Carr, *Cash*, 113.

"solemn, reflective" and "a maturity beyond . . .": Miller, S., *Johnny Cash*, 88.

"From time to . . .": Cash, *Man in Black*, 83.

"twitching and squirming": Cash with Carr, *Cash*, 193.

"Then I had . . .": Cash with Carr, *Cash*, 193.

"burdened down with . . .": Cash, *Man in Black*, 84.

"I dare you . . .": Cash, *Man in Black*, 95.

"By moonlight . . . I . . .": Cash, *Man in Black*, 96.

"hotter than a two-dollar . . .": Miller, S., *Johnny Cash*, 96.

"Cash tied it . . .": McCall, *Johnny Cash*, 59–60.

"I'm making a bomb.": Wren, *Winners Got Scars Too*, 110.

"had been living . . .": Turner, *The Man Called CASH*, 83.

"miserable streak": Campbell, *Johnny Cash*, 108.

"locked within the . . .": Wren, *Winners Got Scars Too*, 131.

CHAPTER SEVEN

"We're on a bombing . . .": Cash, *Man in Black*, 97.

"[We're] going to . . .": Cash, *Man in Black*, 97.

"He was wise . . .": Cash, *Man in Black*, 99.

"I had gone . . .": Cash, *Man in Black*, 103.

"For all practical . . .": Cash with Carr, *Cash*, 99.

"We might have . . .": Cantine, "The Statler Brothers—History of Success," in *The Statler Brothers "Un-Official Home Page."*

"the most influential . . .": Cash with Carr, *Cash*, 185.

"Sit down . . .": Wren, *Winners Got Scars Too*, 154.

"You and I . . .": Cash with Carr, *Cash*, 212.

"Well, good. I . . .": Cash with Carr, *Cash*, 213.

"And there went . . ." Cash with Carr, *Cash*, 213.

"an official welcome": Campbell, *Johnny Cash*, 131.

"Lord, what are . . .": Campbell, *Johnny Cash*, 131.

"Don't worry, June . . .": Campbell, *Johnny Cash*, 131.

"initiation ceremony": Campbell, *Johnny Cash*, 131.

"It was awful . . .": McCall, *Johnny Cash*, 72.

"If you weren't . . .": Campbell, *Johnny Cash*, 135.

"You'd miss me.": Campbell, *Johnny Cash*, 135.

CHAPTER EIGHT

"barely able to . . .": Urbanski, *The Man Comes Around*, 65.

"I meant every . . .": McCall, *Johnny Cash*, 78.

"wallow in their . . .": McCall, *Johnny Cash*, 78.

"Shut up and . . .": Miller, S., *Johnny Cash*, 133.

"dark, bad places": Cash with Carr, *Cash*, 39.

"I was hard . . .": Cash with Carr, *Cash*, 208.

heavy load of . . . : Cash with Carr, *Cash*, 265.

"But you got . . .": Cash, *Man in Black*, 122.

"prayer warrior": Cash with Carr, *Cash*, 226.

"with all her . . .": Cash with Carr, *Cash*, 226.

"walking vision of . . .": Cash with Carr, *Cash*, 229.

"marrow of sadness": Ratliff, "Cash, Back," in *Ring of Fire*, 263.

"Daddy is sick . . .": Cash, *Man in Black*, 104.

"I thought I'd . . .": Cash with Carr, *Cash*, 231.

"dope": Cash, *Man in Black*, 124.

"amphetamine insanity": Cash with Carr, *Cash*, 150.

"He was out . . .": Wren, *Winners Got Scars Too*, 206.

"every breath was . . .": Cash, *Man in Black*, 130.

"the ragin, screamin' . . .": Wren, *Winners Got Scars Too*, 210.

"hold out" and "get better": Cash, *Man in Black*, 210.

CHAPTER NINE

"June, will you . . ." "Let's go on with the show." "Yes! Say yes." and
    "Yes. Yes, I will.": McCall, *Johnny Cash*, 112.

"In short . . . [Johnny's] one of them . . .": Urbanski, *The Man
    Comes Around*, 81.

"You'll feel the single . . .": Cash, Album notes, *Johnny Cash at
    Folsom Prison*, with permission of Sony BMG Music Entertain-
    ment.

"staggering and fumbling . . .": Cash, *Man in Black*, 160.

"hounds of hell": Cash, *Man in Black*, 161.

"with some chords . . .": McCusker, "Johnny Cash—At San
    Quentin," in *CD Times*.

"were standing up . . .": Urbanski, *The Man Comes Around*, 83–84.

"With . . . songs that . . .": Arnowitz, "Music Behind the Bars," in
    LIFE, 12.

"That's a whole different . . .": Miller, S., *Johnny Cash*, 184.

"Sometimes . . . I can . . .": Cash with Carr, *Cash*, 300.

"Johnny Cash if . . .": Miller, S., *Johnny Cash*, 214.

CHAPTER TEN

"Do it your . . .": McCall, *Johnny Cash*, 162.

"survived 12 marriages . . .": McCall, *Johnny Cash*, 174.

"When I got . . .": Cash with Carr, *Cash*, 240.

"They didn't know . . .": Cash with Carr, *Cash*, 243.

"an ongoing struggle": Cash with Carr, *Cash*, 248.

"shipwrecked, beaten with . . .": Cash with Carr, *Johnny Cash*, 312.

"I wanted some . . .": Cash with Carr, *Cash*, 312.

"Johnny Cash didn't . . .": Kirby, "Tale of an artistic turning point," *Chicago Tribune*.

"He's slipping! He's . . .": Cash with Carr, *Johnny Cash*, 351.

"When death starts . . .": Cash with Carr, *Johnny Cash*, 369.

CHAPTER ELEVEN

"I have always . . .": Turner, *The Man Called CASH*, 194. By permission of Rick Rubin and his agents, Ziffren, Brittenham, Branca, et al.

"Johnny Cash, Austerely . . .": Pareles, "Johnny Cash, Austerely Direct from Deep Within," *The New York Times*.

"Cash Conquers": Dickinson, "Cash Conquers," in *Ring of Fire*, x.

"Chordless in Gaza . . .": Tosches, "Chordless in Gaza: The Second Coming of John R. Cash," in *Ring of Fire*, ix.

"Johnny Cash: American . . .": DeYoung, "Johnny Cash: American Music Legend," in *Ring of Fire*, x.

"tales of darkness and . . .": Campbell, *Johnny Cash*, 161.

"John Cash . . .": Tosches, "Chordless in Gaza: The Second Coming of John R. Cash," in *Ring of Fire*, 245.

"It is one . . .": Dowling, "How Johnny Cash got hip," BBC News.

"into what you . . .": Goldstein, "Johnny Cash, 'Something Rude Showing,'" in *Ring of Fire*, 89.

"He's faced a lot . . .": Miller, S., *Johnny Cash*, 354

"Is that you . . .": Miller, S., *Johnny Cash*, 354.

"my rock, my . . .": McCall, *Johnny Cash*, 214.

"The two were . . ." Turner, *The Man Called CASH*, 218.

"were two kinds . . .": Urbanski, *The Man Comes Around*, 182–3.

"so severe, there . . ." McCall, *Johnny Cash*, 214.

"Cash flat out . . .": Urbanski, *The Man Comes Around*, 168.

"A century from . . .": Urbanski, *The Man Comes Around*, 168.

"was the vocal . . .": Holden, "Johnny Cash . . .," *The New York Times*.

"He strengthened . . . the bonds . . .": Holden, "Johnny Cash . . .," *The New York Times*.

"more than wise . . .": McCall, *Johnny Cash*, 25.

"He was a . . .": McCall, *Johnny Cash*, 21.

"He had such . . .": Cave, Nick, quoted in BBC News, "BBC ON THIS DAY, 12 September 2003."

BIBLIOGRAPHY

Arnowitz, Alfred G. "Music Behind the Bars." *LIFE*, August 16, 1968, 12.

BBC News. "ON THIS DAY," September 12, 2003. http://news. bbc.co.uk/onthisday/hi/dates/stories/september/12/newsid_ 3595000/3595300.stm

Campbell, Garth. *Johnny Cash: He Walked the Line, 1932–2003*. London: John Blake Publishing Ltd., 2003.

Cantine, Pam. "The Statler Brothers—History of Success." *The Statler Brothers "Un-Official Home Page."* http://home.twcny. rr.com/statlerbrothers/history.html.

Carr, Patrick. "Cash Comes Back." In *Ring of Fire: The Johnny Cash Reader*, edited by Michael Streissguth. Cambridge, Mass.: Da Capo Press, 2002.

Cash, Johnny. *Man in Black*. New York: Warner Books, 1976.

———. *Man in White*. San Francisco: Harper & Row Publishers, 1986.

Cash, Johnny, with Patrick Carr. *Cash: The Autobiography.* New York: HarperPaperbacks, 1997.

Cash, June Carter. *From the Heart.* New York: Prentice Hall Press, 1987.

Editors of Country Weekly. *Johnny Cash: An American Original.* Nashville: Country Music Media Group, Inc., 2004.

Dearmore, Tom. "First Angry Man of Country Singers." *New York Times Magazine,* September 21, 1969.

DeYoung, Bill. "Johnny Cash: American Music Legend." In *Ring of Fire: The Johnny Cash Reader,* edited by Michael Streissguth. Cambridge, Mass.: Da Capo Press, 2002.

Dickinson, Chris. "Cash Conquers." In *Ring of Fire: The Johnny Cash Reader,* edited by Michael Streissguth. Cambridge, Mass.: Da Capo Press, 2002.

Dolan, Sean. *Johnny Cash.* New York: Chelsea House Publishers, 1995.

Dowling, Stephen. "How Johnny Cash got hip." *BBC News,* UK Edition, Friday, 12 September 2003. http://news.bbc.co.uk/1/hi/entertainment/music/3103700.stm.

Goldstein, Richard. "Johnny Cash, 'Something Rude Showing.'" In *Ring of Fire: The Johnny Cash Reader,* edited by Michael Streissguth. Cambridge, Mass.: Da Capo Press, 2002.

Holden, Stephen. "Johnny Cash, Country Music's Bare-Bones Realist, Dies at 71." *The New York Times,* September 12, 2003.

Kirby, David. "Tale of an Artistic Turning Point." *Chicago Tribune*, Chicago Final Edition, September 12, 2004.

Mansfield, Brian. *Ring of Fire: A Tribute to Johnny Cash*. Nashville: Rutledge Hill Press, 2003.

McCall, Michael. *Johnny Cash: An American Legend*. Boca Raton, Florida: American Media, Inc., 2003.

McCusker, Eamonn. "Johnny Cash—At San Quentin." *CD Times*, December 10, 2003. http://www.cdtimes.co.uk/content.php?contentid=66.

Miller, Bill. *Cash: An American Man*. New York: Pocket Books, 2004.

Miller, Stephen. *Johnny Cash: The Life of an American Icon*. New York: Omnibus Press, 2003.

Pareles, Jon. "Johnny Cash, Austerely Direct from Deep Within," *The New York Times*, September 16, 1994.

Nashville Banner review of "I Walk the Line," July 1956.

Ratliff, Ben. "Cash, Back." In *Ring of Fire: The Johnny Cash Reader*, edited by Michael Streissguth. Cambridge, Mass.: Da Capo Press, 2002.

The editors of *Rolling Stone*. *Cash*. New York: Crown Publishers, 2004.

Sakol, Jeannie. *The Wonderful World of Country Music*. New York: Grossett & Dunlap, 1979.

Tosches, Nick. "Chordless in Gaza: The Second Coming of John R. Cash." In *Ring of Fire: The Johnny Cash Reader*, edited by Michael Streissguth. Cambridge, Mass.: Da Capo Press, 2002.

Turner, Steve. *The Man Called CASH*. Nashville: W Publishing Group, 2004.

Urbanski, Dave. *The Man Comes Around: The Spiritual Journey of Johnny Cash*. Lake Mary, Florida: Relevant Books, 2003.

Wren, Christopher S. *Winners Got Scars Too: The Life and Legends of Johnny Cash*. New York: Ballantine, 1971.

INDEX

PERMISSIONS

The author is grateful for permission to quote from the following sources:

"Music Behind Bars" by Alfred G. Arnowitz, *LIFE* magazine. Copyright © 1968 Time Inc., reprinted by permission.

"He's faced a lot of challenges in his life": Miller, S., *Johnny Cash*, 354, with permission of Lou Robin (Johnny Cash's manager.).

"I have always been drawn to things that are edgy and extreme . . ." and "John Cash is real. In show business . . .": by permission of Rick Rubin and his agents, Ziffren, Brittenham, Branca, et al.

Johnny Cash, He Walked the Line, 1932–2003 by Garth Campbell. Copyright © 2003 John Blake Publishing Ltd.

Cash: The Autobiography by Johnny Cash with Patrick Carr. Copyright © 1997 John R. Cash. Reprinted by permission of HarperCollins Publishers Inc.

Man in Black by Johnny Cash. Copyright © 1976 by Warner Books. Reprinted by permission of Lou Robin (Johnny Cash's manager), representing the Johnny Cash estate.

Johnny Cash: An American Legend by Michael McCall. Copyright © 2003 American Media Books, Inc. Reprinted with permission.

Johnny Cash: The Life of an American Icon written by Stephen Miller. Copyright © 2003 Omnibus Press. Used by permission of Omnibus Press. All rights reserved. International Copyright Secured.

Cash, by the editors of *Rolling Stone*. Copyright © 2004 Crown Publishers (A division of Random House, Inc.).

Ring of Fire: The Johnny Cash Reader by Michael Streissguth. Copyright © 2002 by Michael Streissguth. Reprinted by permission of Da Capo, a member of Perseus Books, L.L.C.

"Chordless in Gaza: The Second Coming of John R. Cash," by Nick Tosches. Copyright © 1955. Used by permission of the author and his agents, Scovil Chichak Galen, Inc.

The Man Comes Around: The Spiritual Journey of Johnny Cash by Dave Urbanski. Copyright © 2003 Relevant Books (A division of Relevant Media Group, Inc).

Johnny Cash at Folsom Prison album notes. Columbia Records 1968. With Permission of Sony BMG Music Entertainment.

LYRICS

"A Boy Named Sue" words and music by Shel Silverstein. Copyright © 1969 (renewed) Evil Eye Music, Inc., Madison, WI. Used by permission.

"Ballad of Ira Hayes" by Peter LaFarge. Copyright © 1962, 1964 Edward B. Marks Music Company. Copyright renewed. Used by permission.

"Big River" Written by John R. Cash. Copyright © 1958, 1986.

House of Cash, Inc. (BMI)/Administered by BUG. All rights reserved. Used by Permission.

"Cry, Cry, Cry" Written by John R. Cash. Copyright © 1955, 1983. House of Cash, Inc. (BMI)/Administered by BUG. All rights reserved. Used by Permission.

"Don't Take Your Guns to Town" Written by Neville Beckford. Basement Music, LTC. (PRS)/Administered by BUG. All rights reserved. Used by Permission.

"Five Feet High and Rising" by Johnny R. Cash. Copyright © 1959 (renewed) Chappell & Co., Inc. All rights reserved. Used by permission. Warner Brothers Publications, Miami, Florida 33014.

"Folsom Prison Blues" Written by John R. Cash. Copyright © 1956, 1984. House of Cash, Inc. (BMI)/Administered by BUG. All rights reserved. Used by Permission.

"Give My Love to Rose" Written by John R. Cash. Copyright © 1957, 1985. House of Cash, Inc. (BMI)/Administered by BUG. All rights reserved. Used by Permission.

"Hey, Porter" Written by John R. Cash. Copyright © 1957, 1985. House of Cash, Inc. (BMI)/Administered by BUG. All rights reserved. Used by Permission.

Lyric excerpt from "Hurt" written by Trent Reznor. All rights reserved. Reprinted by permission of Leaving Hope Music, Inc.

"I Still Miss Someone" Written by John R. Cash and Roy Cash, Jr. Copyright © 1958, 1986. House of Cash, Inc.

(BMI)/Administered by BUG. All rights reserved. Used by Permission.

"I Walk the Line" Written by John R. Cash. Copyright © 1956, 1984. House of Cash, Inc. (BMI)/Administered by BUG. All rights reserved. Used by Permission.

"I'll Fly Away" by Albert E. Brumley. Copyright © 1932 in "Wonderful Message" by Hartford Music Co. Renewed 1960 by Albert E. Brumley & Sons/SESAC (admin. by ICG). All rights reserved. Used by permission.

"Man in Black" Written by John R. Cash. Copyright © 1971, 1998. Song of Cash, Inc. (ASCAP)/Administered by BUG. All rights reserved. Used by Permission.

"Ring of Fire" words and music by Merle Kilgore and June Carter. Copyright © 1962, 1963 Painted Desert Music Corporation, New York. Copyright renewed. International Copyright secured. All rights reserved. Used by permission.

"San Quentin" Written by John R. Cash. Copyright © 1969, 1997. House of Cash, Inc. (BMI)/Administered by BUG. All rights reserved. Used by Permission.

"There Will Be Peace in the Valley for Me" by Thomas Dorsey. Copyright © 1939 (Renewed) by Warner–Tamerlane Publishing Corp. Lyrics reprinted by permission of Alfred Publishing Co., Inc.

"Train of Love" Written by John R. Cash. Copyright © 1957, 1984. House of Cash, Inc. (BMI)/Administered by BUG. All rights reserved. Used by Permission.

FREE PUBLIC LIBRARY UNION NEW JERSEY

3 9549 00388 0763